HOLLY LISLE

MUGGING THE MUSE

Writing Fiction for

Love AND Money

SECOND EDITION

Published by Holly Lisle

Print Version: 978-1475017496
Cover Design: Holly Lisle
Cover Art:	Butterfly Net © Igor Terehkov/ Bigstock.com
		Pink Fairy © Kathy Gold/ Bigstock.com

Holly's Author Photo: © Holly Lisle
Copyright © 2000, 2012 by Holly Lisle

ALL RIGHTS RESERVED

Most of the articles in this book appear on my website, updated here to reflect current publishing reality.

Without limiting the rights under copyright reserved above, no part of this book may be reproduced in any form or by any electronic or mechanical means, including information storage and retrieval systems, without permission in writing from the publisher, except by a reviewer, who may quote brief passages in a review.

DISCLAIMER AND/OR LEGAL NOTICES:

The information in this course has been built from my life and experiences, and it is what works for me. While I have made every effort to translate the decidedly quirky workings of one human mind into a process that will be applicable and accessible to other human minds, I cannot guarantee that this course will work for you, or that my processes will be applicable to your needs and purposes. Nor can I guarantee your success. This course is not intended as a source of legal, accounting, medical or other advice, and is written for information purposes only. While every attempt has been made to verify the information in this course, mistakes happen, and I make them. I will not assume responsibility for errors, inaccuracies, or omissions. I reserve the right to alter and update this course as my processes change, as I learn new things, and as I improve existing methods.

Preface: January, 2000 v

And Another Preface: March, 2012 vi

STOP! You Get Worksheets, Too! viii

The Writing Notebook ix

SECTION I Preparation: Mind and Soul
1

Everyday Courage and the Writer 3

How I Found Myself Here, or Why I Became a Writer 7

Could VS. Should and the Price Of Your Dreams 10

Finding Silence 13

Do Writers Need College to Write? 16

Money From Nothing: The Economic Value of Writing Original Fiction 21

Writing With Integrity: Why Everyone SHOULDN'T Like You 27

Apples, Bananas: The Writer's Need for Experience 32

One Good Enemy 37

How to Tell Who WON'T Make It in Writing (and How Not to Be That Writer) 42

QUIZ: Are You Right for Writing? 48

SECTION II Practice: The Workshops
59

Creating Conflict, or The Joys of Boiling Oil 61

Scene Creation Workshop: Writing Scenes that Move Your Story Forward 67

The Character Workshop: Designing A Life 73

Deeper People: Putting Yourself Into Your Characters 75

Notecarding: Plotting Under Pressure 80

The Description Workshop 87

Pacing Dialogue and Action Scenes: Your Story at Your Speed 95

Maps Workshop: Developing the Fictional World Through Mapping 102

The Magic of Goals: How to Get There from Here 107

SECTION III Writing & Selling
119

Your Book Is Not Your Baby 121

Say What You Mean 124

The Writer's Toolbox 129

Finding Your Themes 131

Ten Steps to Finding Your Writing Voice 135

How to Finish a Novel 143

How to Collaborate, And How Not To 149

How to Query an Agent or Editor 155

SECTION IV Frequently Asked Questions
161

The FAQs (Frequently Asked Questions) About Self-Publishing 163

The FAQs About How to Write 173

FAQs About Money 180

FAQs About the Business of Writing 193

My Three Most Frequently Asked Questions 200

My Five Worst Career Mistakes, and How You Can Avoid Them 202

Ten Keys to Designing A Series Character You Can Live With (Forever) 212

How to Make Every Story Better Than the Last 218

Final Thoughts 222

About the Author 225

My Writing Courses 227

My Novels, Short Stories, and More 228

Preface:
January, 2000

I've been self-supporting as a novelist since the end of 1992. I won't say that I've always managed to support my family in style, but I've never had to quit writing and get a day job in order to feed us. Writing is a challenging profession — writing fiction full-time is an exercise in lunacy. But it's great fun, and if it's something you've always hungered for, read on. This is how I do it, and how you can do it, too.

Holly Lisle

January, 2000

And Another Preface:
March, 2012

(Because one just ain't enough...)

Things change. Things change a lot, and the changes in publishing in the last twelve years have been stunning. In 1998, I pitched this book to my agent, who shot it down because, he said, the only publisher interested in books on writing fiction was Writer's Digest, and Writer's Digest didn't pay well.

In 2000, I wrote the book anyway because I discovered I could create PDFs on my computer, and there was a place where I could sell them: BookLocker.com.

This book in its first incarnation stayed on the BookLocker.com bestseller list — priced at right around ten dollars — from the day it debuted until the day I removed it from Booklocker because Booklocker was switching its model to epublishing plus print, and suddenly required books published there to be in both formats — and I couldn't afford the fees they were charging to put the book into print format.

So I put *Mugging the Muse* up on my own site and gave it away in PDF format.

Twelve years, and thousands upon thousands upon thousands of downloads later, however, it occurred to me that things **had** changed in the publishing industry, and that this book could probably use an update.

Better yet, there were new ways to read it that were far better than PDF, and I now had at my fingertips the technology to present the book in those formats.

Plus, I needed to include some information on self-publishing and self-promotion, which are the best thing to happen to writers since...hmm...the invention of paper?...the typewriter?...the personal computer?.... Those are all wonderful, but being able to reach readers directly is *better*.

I needed to remove a few chapters that were painfully out of date. I needed to go through the articles that remained and add a few necessary annotations and comments.

I added some new chapters, covering issues that didn't even exist when the first version of this book came out.

AND I wanted to include some extra writing workshops, of which the *First Edition* of *Mugging the Muse* only had three.

Finally, I added a little writing exercise to the end of each chapter — because if you want to do this for a living, you'd better like to write — but also because if you want to do this, you need to figure out HOW you're going to make it happen, and WHY you want to do it.

So get a little spiral-bound notebook and answer the question at the end of each chapter as you read through the book. You'll learn a lot by doing this. I promise.

Mugging the Muse is now *Second Edition*. Bigger, better, *interactive*...and once again current.

Write with joy.

Holly Lisle

March 6, 2012

STOP! You Get Worksheets, Too!

This course includes downloadable, printable worksheets that support the Section Two Workshop lessons.

Before you start, create your free account on my site and get your PDF worksheets.

http://HowToThinkSideways.com/join-us

You'll receive a confirmation email with your login information and password, so make sure before you submit your information that you do not have any typos or errors in your e-mail address.

Some free email providers, **among them AOL, Hotmail, and Yahoo mail,** frequently delete auto-generated emails rather than delivering them.

If you use one of these addresses to create your account, be aware that you may not receive your login email, and the only solution is to use a different email provider and create a new account with a different user name.

If you require free email, my students have had good delivery results with Gmail.

You may also want to explore other free email alternatives:

http://www.fepg.net/emailtypes.html

Once you've registered and logged in, you'll see the link for your *Mugging the Muse* worksheet downloads, along with worksheet downloads for several of my other writing courses, under the WORKSHEET DOWNLOADS header on your student page. (You're welcome to download all of them.)

"Can I print out the worksheets so everyone in my writer's group can do the exercises together?"

Yes, you may.

If you'd rather not foot the whole bill for paper and printer toner every week, though, you can suggest each member spend the 99 cents to get their own copy of the ebook and the free worksheets, and bring their worksheets with them to the meeting.

(Yes, I'll make an extra 25 cents or so per person if you do this. You, on the other hand, will save a couple bucks for the ream of paper and the toner. I used to print stuff for my writer's group. I know how expensive it can be.)

The Writing Notebook

You're going to need a writing notebook. You don't need anything fancy or expensive. I buy notebooks anyplace that sells the 5"x7" wire-bound 80-sheet lined paper versions. WalMart and Target always have them, while office supply stores frequently don't. I like the kind with the elastic band on the back to keep the notebook closed in my purse. You may not need this feature.

But get used to carrying a notebook with you, with your pen tucked into the wire binding. If you're a writer, you'll use it for much more than this course.

SECTION I
Preparation: Mind and Soul

In this section, you'll find out what it means to write for a living, and discover why you want to write, what tools you can build to help you write better, and how to make the transition from wanting to write into being a writer.

Have your writing notebook handy. You'll be answering questions that will help you direct yourself into the mindset of the professional writer.

Everyday Courage and the Writer

Back when I was attending a fair number of conventions and signing a decent number of books, I came up with a saying which I attributed to my Hoos headhunters from the Arhel books, and called a Hoos proverb. It was, "Courage is nothing more than taking one step more than you think you can."

Neither the proverb nor the sentiment are particularly original, but I have no idea who said the words first, or how he might have said them. I do know the words are true. Courage has nothing to do with feeling or not feeling fear, with doing great deeds (though sometimes courage accomplishes great deeds), or with conquering life-and-death situations (though in such situations it is certainly helpful.)

Courage is a form of tenaciousness, a refusal to quit when you want to quit because you're tired or humiliated or broken, and it is as necessary in everyday life as it is in moments of great upheaval. In fact, I could easily say that everyday courage is *more* important than the 'great deeds' sort, because every one of us will be in everyday situations, while not all of us will be called upon in our lifetimes to perform great deeds.

Courage is as essential to the writer as oxygen, no more and no less. The writer who lacks courage will never succeed.

And you're saying, "That's silly. I can't think of a safer sort of work."

Really? Think again.

Let me define what writing is for you. You're going to attempt to sell the products of your mind to a world that doesn't care right now whether you breathe or not. You're going to strip your soul naked and parade it in front of editors and agents, publishers and eventually — if you're persistent and lucky and talented — readers. You're going to say "What I carry around inside my head is so interesting, so compelling, so riveting, that you, the agent, are going to want to risk your reputation with editors for being a shrewd judge of talent to present the products of my fancy to them; and that you, the editor, are going to want to put your career on the line to fight to bring my imaginings to press; and that you, the publisher are going to want to spend tens or hundreds of thousands of dollars presenting these imaginings to a world that has never heard of me; and that you, the reader, are going to want to put your hard-earned money on the line so that I can tell you a story that will give you nothing tangible."

While you are reaching out to editors, agents and publishers, you're going to fail. Over and over and over again, you are going to send things out and they are going to come back with impersonal rejection notices, with no notices at all, with the occasional signed memo that "This isn't for us." You are going to stare at your words and sit in a darkened room and wonder, "What the hell is the matter with me?" You are going to take the rejections personally, are going to hurt, are going to bleed. Agents will turn you down, editors will turn you down, places that don't even pay for stories will turn you down.

So say you have courage. Say you go on, and you take one step more than you think you can, and then one step more after that, and then one step more after that. Eventually you will sell something. You'll get paid. You'll 'succeed.' Your story or your book will enter the marketplace, and maybe you'll do well with it, or maybe you won't. In either case, let's say you keep going. You sell again.

Or perhaps you'll decide to publish your work yourself, skipping the pain and frustration of dealing with publishers. In that case, along with writing your book, you will either do your own cover art, layout, formatting, editing and copyediting, uploading, selling, and promoting, or you'll pay someone else to do these things. Either way, you are investing in yourself — in your ability to know what is good, in your ability to tell a story worth reading, in your ability to reach readers directly and entertain them enough that they will not only like your first effort, but like it enough to search out your later works. Again, if you focus on your craft, learn what it takes to write a good story, and learn how to make sure your work is presentable when you send it out into the world, you will eventually succeed.

Even though you've succeeded, you're going to fail some more. You'll get hostile reviews. Letters from people who don't think you can write. Comments from critics questioning your talent, your vocation, your species. These will, if you're lucky, come interspersed with glowing reviews, a nice sell-through, an offer from your editor to buy the next thing you're doing, but don't think for a minute that the good things will offset the pain of the bad. They run in parallel courses, these good and bad responses, and they don't touch each other's worlds at all. I'm always delighted by the good reviews, always hurt by the bad ones.

But go on. You take another few steps, and these seem easier. You do more books, find an audience, settle into a flow. You discover one of the ugly facts of success — that there are people who you thought were your friends who were only your friends when you were failing. Now that you have, in their eyes, reached success, you have become the enemy. A target. They want to see you fall down, because when you are standing, you make them feel their own failures more.

You leave the false friends behind. You keep writing, keep selling, get fan mail, generate some nice reviews, make guest appearances at conventions, become (as much as any writer ever does) a celebrity in your field. And somewhere along the way you realize that you want to stretch your wings. Try something you haven't tried before. You write this new thing, and your fans hate it because it's different, and your editor takes a beating, and your publisher loses money, and all of a sudden you're in a precarious position. You have to decide — pursue the new course and take chances, or stagnate in the old thing that has become popular and that is starting to feel like a prison. Or find some third writing course.

All along the way, you've had to face the certainty of various sorts of failure. You've been embarrassed by your family, who does not understand why you must do this ridiculous thing. You've felt pain and rejection and worthlessness. You've had your soul and your talent and your hope stepped on, and you've cried your share of private tears, and you've kept up a brave face in public more than you'll ever admit. Even when you succeed by your own definition of success, whatever that might be, you will continue to struggle, and you will never leave the struggle behind. Every story and every book is another chance to fail just exactly as much as it is another chance to succeed. Every new level of success raises the bar higher, making failure more public and more painful ... and more likely. Every day is a challenge, and every day requires courage.

I've learned this about writing — if you will not put yourself in a position to fail, you cannot succeed. The two are as inseparably linked as breathing in is linked to breathing out. You cannot have one without the other, though you can live a safe life and have neither.

Courage is standing at the bottom of the mountain, knowing that the climb is going to hurt like hell and that you might never reach the top, and climbing anyway. Courage is saying "One more step. Just one more step," when hands and knees and heart are bleeding. Courage is saying that you might let yourself quit tomorrow, but that you're going to hang in today, just for now… and not telling your tired, hurting self that the next day is always today, and the next moment is always now.

What about my climb? I've done my share of falling, and I have the scars to show for it. It seems like there's as much mountain above me as there ever was, though when I look back, I can see that I've covered a surprising amount of ground, every bit of it one step at a time. I still don't know what the view from the top is like. I do know what the view from the first ledge above the treeline is like, though, and it's been worth the climb so far. I'm still working my way up the mountain, because what you can see from up here is nothing you can even get pictures of in the valley where it's safe. Part of the beauty, I think, comes from having survived the pain. Part of the elation, too. If it were easy, it wouldn't be any fun.

This is the world of writing, and it is the *only* world of writing. Every writer climbs the same mountain, though we all climb it by our own path. You can make this climb. It takes courage, but it only takes the sort of courage everybody can have — the courage not to quit when quitting would be the easy thing to do. You will not be called on to perform heroics — to leap into burning buildings or lift cars or fling yourself into the midst of a shark feeding frenzy to save a drowning child. All you have to do is take one more step. Remember to keep your head up, brush the dirt off your face and pick the gravel out of your palms when you fall, and know that every other person who climbed the mountain has done the same thing.

Good luck in your climb. My wish for you is this: May you have the courage to fail, because it is the courage to succeed.

EXERCISE: Answer the following question in between 100 and 250 words:

What scares me the most when I consider writing for a living, and WHY does it scare me?

How I Found Myself Here, or Why I Became a Writer

I didn't set out to be a writer. I always wrote, you know, but it was just this thing I did; what I intended was to become a terribly famous artist, perhaps with a stopover as a singer. And I can't say I made much of a go at that. I got out of high school, and didn't go to college. My folks had spent most of their lives telling me that college was a waste of time and money, and that what I needed to do was get out of school and get a job. And in spite of the fact that I graduated in the top ten in my class (not top ten percent — top ten) and had taken all college preparatory classes, I believed them.

Which turns out not to have been the only stupid mistake I made in my life that turned out well. For the record, college is a good idea for many people, and if I still had my heart set on being a professional artist, it would have been important for me. Singing...well, that takes more talent than I have, and I never wanted it enough to fight for it anyway. I had my moment in the spotlight there and that was enough.

But getting out of school and getting a job is what you do when your life has other plans for you, and just hasn't let you in on them yet. I discovered that the world is not panting in breathless anticipation for eighteen-year-old high-school-graduate artists.

So I started to work at a newspaper, selling advertising. I found out quickly that I don't like working for other people — -but I also acquired a little Vega station wagon that had to be paid for. When selling advertising turned out not to be my dream job, I dumped it for the first art job that came along.

I began painting signs for a commercial artist, and discovered *that* entailed working in a cold warehouse and dealing with people who hadn't been paid by this guy in months, and smelling kerosene all the time, and getting chapped fingers and chapped lips and paint in the cracks that the turpentine and the cold made in my hands.

So I started teaching guitar at a local music shop, and while I was at it, picked up a couple of gigs at local restaurants as a singer. What I found from these jobs was that I was working lots of hours for not a lot of money, and if I ever wanted to move out of my parents' house (and I did, let me tell you) I was going to have to do something that paid regular money, and a fair amount of it. I added McDonald's, so that technically I had three jobs at the same time (teaching beginner guitar, singing in restaurants, and saying, "Would you like fries with that?" but while I was sure as hell employed, I wasn't making enough money to feed a dieting cockroach.

My mother (who also wanted me out of the house sometime in her lifetime) was working at a local hospital. She ran into some of the nursing students there, and came home from work one day and told me I ought to go to nursing school. It was cheap, it was local, and the uniforms were cute. (They were also polyester and hot as hell, but they were, indeed, cute.)

So I went to the technical institute, boned up on algebra, and took the test. I passed easily, and found myself at the very top of what was for some people a two year waiting list. And with about that much forethought, I started into two years of hell as a nursing student, where I discovered that the uniforms might have been cute but the work wasn't. I discovered more than that, though. I discovered the enormous variety of humanity, and life and death, and pain, and hope, and love and hate and fear.

Ten years of nursing following that put me in touch with the basic themes of my life. That people matter. That love and our time are all we have to offer each other that means anything. That death is a mean bastard, and that he comes for all of us. That life is worth living, no matter how painful or scary it sometimes gets. That magic is real.

That I hate the assholes who gravitate to administration.

Yeah, well...not all themes are uplifting. I had to get out of nursing. The patients and the actual work were wonderful, but the paperwork was bullshit, and I don't know where hospitals dig up the creatures who end up as administrators and head nurses, but I swear, they need to bury them back where they found them and hire humans for the job.

I'd been writing all along. Short stories, poems, twenty-page "I'm going to write a novel now" false starts. I finally got serious. Writing was how I was going to make my way out of the increasingly bitter world of nursing. And to make a long story a little shorter, I sold my first fantasy novel, *Fire in the Mist*. I sold a couple more. And I quit nursing.

I quit too soon, and I've had to run like hell to keep in one place most of the time since then. But I did it. I'm out of nursing. I work for myself (and I really am about the only person I willingly take orders from). And writing, for all that it's harder than nursing ever was, is also more joyous, and more fun, and a lot less dangerous. And the major themes of my life have become the major themes of my writing, too — so it has all worked out pretty well.

And everything I ever did prepared me better than college ever could have for what I do today. Like I said, this has been a long, hard road, but skipping college was one of the best dumb mistakes I ever made.

EXERCISE: Answer the following question in between 100 and 250 words:

What obstacles have you overcome in your life to get where you are, and what obstacles do you foresee facing as you pursue your dream of writing?

Could VS. Should and the Price Of Your Dreams

A friend of mine is going through a crisis of faith right now. Not a religious crisis. A writing one — though from where he's standing, it probably feels much the same. He's written several books and a slough of short stories, and he has prepared them professionally, and he has diligently and tirelessly sent them around in the correct manner. He's done everything right, and he has a growing collection of rejection slips to show for it, and an upcoming publication in what he calls "the smallest paying market in existence."

And he's starting to wonder why he's doing all this; as he points out, he has a great job that he's lucky enough to like, he's happily married, he makes good money and has what he needs in life. He's putting a lot of time into something that is feeling more and more like smacking himself in the forehead with a ballpeen hammer. Repeatedly.

Is he wasting his time? I have no doubt at all that if he sticks with his writing long enough, he'll start selling his work. He's smart and talented and funny, and I think it would be impossible for him to keep writing without those qualities showing in an irresistible combination on the page eventually. Sooner or later, an editor is going to fall in love, and he is going to find a publishing home.

If he is willing to pay the price.

The price?

Every dream has a price. You need to know this now, because the price can be enormous, and if you don't know about in advance, you can wake up one day to find that you have paid with everything you ever loved, and what you have to show for all of that isn't enough.

How much will you have to pay to be a writer? There's no way you can know in advance. How much might you have to pay?

You might have to live in poverty. You might lose your job, your friends or family, your children or your spouse. Your dream might cost you your health. Your happiness. Your life. Perhaps you think I exaggerate, but writers suffer from depression and die of suicide far out of proportion to our numbers. We have high divorce rates, far too many substance abusers, and as a group we are pathetically poor. I'm not saying that if you want to be a writer, you need to run out and get a divorce and take up heavy drinking. Far from it. A strong, stable relationship can get you through some desperate times. And only fools look for inspiration in the bottom of a bottle. What I am saying is that if you pursue your dream, some other parts of your life *will* fall by the wayside. You can't know what those parts will be yet. But if you persist, you will find out.

How much is your dream worth to you?

Could you be a writer? Yes.

Should you be?

That is a question that only you can answer ... and you'll have to answer it again every time you pay.

But before you walk away, consider this: If writing is your hunger and your thirst, and if you choose not to follow your dream because you're afraid, you'll pay a price for that, too — you'll pay with the progressive deadening of your soul, as time and your own disillusionment with yourself eat away at who you are. One day you'll wake up and discover that the part of yourself that knew how to dream — and how to fly — has died, and that you are forever after bound to the ground, with only the memory that you once had wings.

Every dreamer pays a price. But so does everyone who fears to dream.

EXERCISE: Answer the following questions in between 100 and 250 words:

What is the worst thing that could happen if you become a writer (and how likely is that to happen)?

What is the worst thing that could happen if you DON'T become a writer (and how likely is that to happen)?

Finding Silence

We who write or aspire to write make much of place. A place to work, a room of our own, an office, a nice quiet spot at a corner diner where the waitresses know not to ask how we're doing if the pen is moving ... a place in the world to call *mine*.

We claim this space in the name of writing, and guard it jealously, because space set aside acts to validate our dreams, and reminds us of the promise we have made to ourselves — the promise to write. When we are in our space and writing, spouses need not visit, friends dare not call, children had better be bleeding or the house burning down before they interrupt. I have a place, and I love it.

My office is half of our small spare bedroom, a decent build-it-yourself kit desk, a computer and a comfortable typing chair with a firm back. I have a sliding glass door that looks out on the parking lot of the apartment complex next door, and plastic vertical blinds that don't keep out the sound nearly as well as I'd like when the crazy people in the apartment complex next door are jumping up and down in the parking lot threatening to kill each other. But most of the time, it's a pretty nice office.

Place matters. I hate to think of writing again without it. I've done it before, it wasn't fun, I got away from it as soon as I could and have done everything in my power since to keep from sitting in the living room in the middle of mayhem. But place only matters if we also have the silence to make use of it. And silence is harder to find.

I'm not talking about the sort of silence you get when the kids are at school and the spouse is at work and the phone is set to take messages at the first ring. That sort of silence is fine, but not essential to work. I've worked in the middle of a convention with thousands of people streaming past me on either side, all talking loudly — I knew they were there, but I didn't hear them. And on many occasions I've tried to work in an empty, quiet house, and found that the noise in my mind made productive thought impossible.

The silence I'm talking about, the silence we as writers must have to be productive, is silence inside ourselves. That silence travels anywhere. We carry it with us as if it were a private retreat in the mountains nestled next to a crystalline, ice-cold lake, surrounded by forests and pervaded by peace. And this silence is hard to find and hard to hold. It is as elusive as a rainbow, as easily shattered as sugar glass, as rare as a white stag, as skittish as a wild colt. A single worry about an unpaid bill or an appointment with a dentist or a remembered argument can destroy this silence for an hour or a day, and no amount of gritting teeth and frowning at the monitor with fingers poised on keyboard will lure it back.

I have fought my battles with the noise of the mind, and have lost my own share of time and pages to stupid replays of arguments and fantasies of future greatness and worries that I can do nothing about at the moment. I've gradually come to a place where I've started winning the battle, though, and winning it often enough that I think I'm on to something.

The search for your characters' voices and your story's action and the truth of the world that you are building begins in the silence of your mind. You can reach that silence through training your mind to stillness — not an easy task, but one that offers tremendous rewards. While I'm sure people have found dozens of ways to lead their minds to quiet, I've found that meditation works for me.

I advocate no religious systems and follow none — my meditation is nothing more than sitting cross-legged on the floor, my hands clasped in my lap in front of me and my eyes closed, breathing to a slow count of four. Inhale to four, exhale to four. I slow my breathing and counting as I begin to relax, I acknowledge stray thoughts that wander into my mind and immediately dismiss them, and I sit for fifteen minutes. No more, no less. I have a little timer that I sit in front of me, and I set it to run backwards — I'm to the point now where, when I peek at it, I'm almost always just a few seconds to either side of fifteen minutes, and when my mind has behaved itself for that long, it seems to be long enough. Quieting my conscious mind allows me to hear what my subconscious mind — my Muse — has to say to me.

For the rest of the day while I write, I can reach that silence again with a couple of slow breaths while my eyes are closed. I keep a meditation journal, too, which most days doesn't say anything more than that I sat for fifteen minutes and more or less concentrated on my breathing. Some days in the middle of that lovely silence I have a revelation that electrifies my work. Occasionally while I meditate I break through a wall that has held me stymied. Mostly I just sit, and if I only just sat, it would be enough. Because on the days when I meditate, I invariable finish my allotted number of pages. On the days when I don't, and when my mind wanders and chatters and refuses to shut up, sometimes I still manage to succeed. Sometimes I fail.

Which would make you think that I would never skip a day of meditation voluntarily, wouldn't it? But I do.

Sometimes I get the same benefits from standing under the hot water in the shower — so I skip the meditation.

Sometimes I just skip the meditation anyway. The mind resists being made to behave, and offers all sorts of reasons and enticements and cajoleries for missing a day, or a couple of days, or a week, or a month. 'You don't have the time,' or 'you have to pay bills,' or 'you already know exactly what you want to write today so why don't we just get to it?' Sometimes my mind is convincing enough, and sometimes I am lazy enough, that I skip it. And frequently I regret it.

Finding silence takes discipline, and I'm not always disciplined. It takes commitment, and sometimes I don't have the commitment. It takes living up to a promise I made to myself, and sometimes I don't live up to it.

When I do, I'm better, I'm happier, I'm more productive. And I keep hoping that the next time my noisy mind tries to get me to skip my morning silence, I'll remember that. Perhaps what it really takes is getting smarter. Maybe the silence will eventually even give me that.

EXERCISE: Answer the following question in between 100 and 250 words:

How can you quiet your conscious mind so you can hear what your subconscious mind — your Muse — is trying to tell you?

Do Writers Need College to Write?
Experts, Professionals, and College

"Do I have to have a college education to make it as a writer?" "I haven't finished high school. Can I still write?" "I've always wanted to be a writer, and I've done a lot of writing, but I couldn't afford to go to college when I was younger..." This question arrives in my e-mail box about once a week, worded in any of a dozen different ways. Some of the questioners tiptoe around it, embarrassed to ask, pretty sure they know what the answer is going to be, but hoping that it won't. Sometimes I can feel the frustration and the pain, the barriers erected by poverty or lack of a diploma or lack of time. Some of the questioners are as young as thirteen, some have been as old a seventy.

All of them are pretty sure that formal education is the road to writing; that a degree will confer legitimacy to their words and their lives; that if they could just get more schooling, publishers' doors would open.

They've been brainwashed by experts, by a system designed to create people who fit neatly into categories like 'accountant' and 'nurse' and 'manager'. They've been trained to believe that the best education is an education that comes from sitting passively in a desk in an overcrowded room, being talked at by an expert.

Obviously, experts have gone to a great deal of trouble to make sure their potential customers (and perhaps you) believed this. They've tried to get employers to make grades the basis for hiring — a move most employers have so far been bright enough to refuse. They have managed to close many fields to anyone who hasn't sat in the box like a good little drone for sixteen years or more.

You now have to have a degree to be an architect, a doctor, a teacher, or an engineer. Experts are trying to make sure you have to have a degree to become an RN. They'd also prefer that you had to have a degree in order to be a social worker, respiratory therapist, an interior decorator...and sooner or later, when they make degrees mandatory to those fields, I imagine they'll get to work on truckers and plumbers and bakers and hairdressers. College-educated experts are trying to close every field, because college education is big, pricey business, and the more people that have to go through it, the more money the experts make.

And if you think I'm full of shit here, and that people really do need college educations before going out and doing great things, consider this — the gothic cathedrals, the pyramids, and the Roman roads and aqueducts were designed and built by men who did not have college educations. Michaelangelo did not have a college degree, nor did Leonardo da Vinci. Thomas Edison didn't. Neither did Mark Twain (though he was granted honorary degrees in later life.) All of these people were professionals. None of them were experts.

Get your education from professionals, and always avoid experts.

An expert is somebody with a degree. The degree doesn't mean he knows how to do what he's an expert at — he might have absolutely no practical experience. But he has the degree, which confers on him the right to impress other people with his accomplishment (which was the getting of the degree), and to get paid for his expert opinions. An expert gets paid by third parties — his work is never placed in the open market where it will either sink or swim on its own merit. Experts earn more money and more security by conforming — if they conform for a long enough time without annoying anyone or doing anything unexpected, they can earn higher positions or, in college systems, tenure. Therefore, in an expert system, the talented, the challenging and the brash are weeded out, and the inoffensive mediocre remain. Many college professors are experts.

A professional is someone who makes a living working in the field in question. A professional architect designs and builds houses for clients. A professional hairdresser cuts and styles hair for clients. A professional writer writes stories, articles, or books for readers. All of these people get paid by the people who are direct consumers of their work. If they do bad work, they don't get paid. The open market will weed out the bad professionals, so the ones who have been around for a while and who are still working are probably worth learning from.

What I learned from two years of nursing school at a community college was primarily political — "Get involved in your local chapter of the North Carolina Nursing Association, fight to keep the ANA from making a bachelor's degree the entry level for an RN, don't stand up when doctors come into the nurses' station or give them your seat." I learned some basics on patient care, too — but I didn't really learn to be a nurse until I was out in the field working with other nurses. They were the ones who said, "Look, you see somebody who comes in looking like that, don't wait for the doctor to get here before you stick O2 on him and order a twelve-lead. Just do it. And break out the D5W and start a microdrip IV right away, too. And for Godsake, make sure the crash cart is ready and the paddles are warmed up."

In writing, too, I learned the things I needed to know about the profession from a brief apprenticeship with Mercedes Lackey and another with Stephen Leigh. From Stephen, I learned the nuts and bolts of writing: 1. Avoid passive voice, 2. Use active verbs, 3. Eliminate most adjectives and adverbs, 4. Use concrete detail, 5. Tell a story worth telling, 6. Know your characters. From Misty, I learned how to be a professional — and **that** I learned from watching her. She came home from a full day of work and went straight into her office and wrote her ten pages...every day, no matter what kind of a day she'd had. Only when she'd done that did she come out and hang out. She was invariably polite and friendly to her agent, her editors, her publishers, and her fans. She worked on ideas for one project while writing another. She didn't have a shit fit about having to do rewrites — she just did them. She hit her deadlines. She wrote stories she wanted to write.

There. I've just given you a complete apprenticeship in writing. You have everything you need to know to become a professional writer, and it took you a couple of minutes of your time and didn't cost you a penny. The rest of being a professional writer is writing — sitting down and putting words on a page, one after another after another.

If you want to pay $40,000 or $60,000 or whatever for a college education, you can do that, and perhaps you'll even have one or two professors in your program who are actually working as writers. They aren't doing it full time, of course, because if they were, they wouldn't be supplementing their income by teaching, so you won't be able to model a full-time writer by watching them. You'll have to spend a lot of time doing things that have no relationship to what you want to do with your life. And you need to remember that most people who go to college to become writers don't. They find their focus shifted to education, or business, and they give up on their dream. College educations are designed by conformists to create conformists. Even those colleges which point to their radical stance and avante garde teaching are creating students who conform to their mold — **their** sort of radicals, **their** sort of avante garde. Students in college have to earn the approval of their teachers in order to get their grades and graduate. And you don't learn anything new if your main goal in life is seeking the approval of experts.

If you're looking at writing as a career, you're looking at a future of tremendous freedom. You can do what you want to do with your life, and publishers and editors don't ask if you have a degree, and don't **care** if you have a degree. They only care that you can put good words on a page, and that you can tell a story. They'll pay you well if you can do those two things — and you can learn to do them without a college education, without a high school education, without having spent a day in your life locked behind the walls of a classroom.

You'll learn to write if you teach yourself. Put yourself in situations where you can learn new things from the people who actually do them. Hang out with policemen and painters and long-distance runners and carpenters. Get them to show you the tricks of their trade. Learn how to build a stained glass window, how to paddle a canoe, how to swim, how to bait your own hook and tie your own flies and how to identify the flowers and shrubs and trees native to your region. Grow a garden. Paint your own house and fix your own leaky faucet. Go camping with a couple of outdoorsy friends. Read lots and lots and lots of good books. Read fiction, read non-fiction. Especially read lots of books about complicated subjects written for the intelligent layman.

Never, never pick up a textbook — textbooks are worthless. They're politically correct pablum designed to spoonfeed tiny bits of information to people who aren't interested in the subject matter without offending those people's parents. Anything designed with being inoffensive as its primary goal isn't going to be worth your time — life itself is pretty offensive, ending as it does with death.

And while you're doing all this reading and self-educating, keep writing. Have the guts to believe in yourself, have the guts to ignore the experts who want your money, have the guts to take a chance on making your dream a reality. You can do it.

Am I sure?

Yes, I am.

You see, I'm a full-time professional writer, and I don't have a college education either.

EXERCISE: Answer the following question in between 100 and 250 words:

What have you learned from LIFE that has given you themes, experience, and and ideas for stories you can start telling *right now?*

Money From Nothing: The Economic Value of Writing Original Fiction

A Foray Even Your Mother Will Appreciate Into Why Writing Isn't a Waste of Your Time

From the perspective of feeding the soul, we writers already know we stand upon solid ground.

When we write, we do our own souls good (or at bare minimum, placate our raging ids.) By providing what we have written for others to read, we entertain at least some of the people some of the time — in some cases we do much more, offering encouragement or support that helps a reader figure out how to change the direction of his life, or pull back from pending tragedy, or dare to take chances that will make not just his life but the lives of those around him better.

None of which is particularly useful when you want to sell the idea of you as writer to your folks, your significant other, or your friends.

To the casual observer, unless you're up in the J. K. Rowling/ Stephen King/ Norman Mailer leagues, writing is a fairly worthless hobby.

But it just ain't so.

If you are a writer — even if you are the worst, least successful writer in the world and just doing this on your weekends because you like to — you are a positive force in the economy.

Don't believe me? Then watch.

Say you're horrible.

Say that you're turning out the most gruesome dreck the planet has ever seen, and say that you are never, ever, ever going to get better. You're still doing good things for your corner of the world. You bought notebook and pens or a typewriter or word processor or a computer, you bought software, you bought paper, printer, printer toner, or ribbons and Wite-Out. Somewhere out there, some small portion of the economy thanks your for your steady support of the products above mentioned.

Now, if you go a step further and send out your atrocious manuscript to a place that accepts over-the-transom submissions (and at this point, we're looking almost exclusively at short story markets), you have just been involved in helping to create and maintain a few jobs. Slush-readers and junior editors will get paid in part because you and thousands of others like you wrote dreadful manuscripts that **someone** had to evaluate.

So even the worst writers ever are doing something valuable for someone besides themselves.

But keep going. Let's say you *don't* suck.

Let's say that you've written a passable midlist title that someone, somewhere in the commercial publishing universe, wants to buy. Not only have you created money out of thin air for yourself (anything above the investment you make in supplies and research materials is money you just invented — but can still spend). You didn't take anything from anyone else to create this income. No one else had to lose so you could win. You invented money for yourself by inventing a product someone wanted. And your invention of brand-new money doesn't stop with you.

You have also just exponentially increased your contributions to the world. First off, you are now one of fifteen to fifty writers just like you who have created a paying job for one agent. As more writers need agents, more agents will be able to find work agenting. But that isn't the only job your work makes possible.

You have been cause for the creation or continuation of jobs from junior editor to senior editor to copyeditor to publisher to bookbinder and typesetter to book marketer to bookseller to bookstore owner.

You have employed one artist for one cover painting and are responsible for the existence of a piece of art that would not have existed had you not sat down to write your story. Reviewers would not exist without you and other writers like you. You've created a profit item for corporations, and an ad revenue source for media (if somebody is paying to advertise your book, somebody is being paid to advertise it).

Say you're better than passable. Say your book was good.

Say it does really well for you. You get more of that magic money you made out of nothing but thoughts inside your head. Plus, you start providing work for advertising companies or in-house artists who develop your promo materials. Your sales add a bit to the GNP. The fact that your book made profits for the publisher will allow the publisher to publish other writers who wouldn't have been able to find slots without your successful novel.

What if you self-publish?

What if you skip the agent, the publishing house, the slew of slush readers and junior editors and senior editors and simply put your book out there, and yourself with it?

You're still a huge force for good in the world. You've still created out of your thoughts and your effort something that did not exist before — and **every time** you get paid for it, you have created money that did not exist before. I know it looks like the same old money that was floating around in folks' pockets already. **But it ISN'T.** When you create something new that has value, the economy expands by the exact value of the thing you've created. How much value is that? Add it up as it comes in and see.

Part of this money will go directly to you (and that, my friend, is *sweeeeet*). Part will go to the online shops that offer your work, so you're helping them stay in business and present the work of other writers like you as well as you. Part will go to anyone you employed directly — from an editor to a proofreader to the guy who designed your cover. If you use Lulu or CreateSpace to create hard copies of your work, every time someone buys one of those, you've taken a positive step toward keeping jobs available for people who plant trees and mill them and make paper and make bindings and print your cover and make the glue that keeps the cover on the book and packages the book to send to your new reader.

You. Did. That. And that's a good thing.

But there's more. Lots more.

Say your good book (whether self-pubbed or commercially published) sells in foreign countries. Now you're creating jobs for translators, more editors and agents and typesetters and bookbinders and bookseller and distributors. You are a benefit to the international economy, you are a benefit to various national economies, and in a way you have the potential to be an envoy for your own country. Depends on what you wrote. Still, the possibility is there.

We're not done yet. Think big thoughts.

Now you sell story rights to a motion picture company. You're still a benefit to all the people you've already helped, but now you're **also** providing work for everyone from the people who scout filming locations (and money for the areas that permit filming in those locations) to set designers and prop creators and screenwriters, to camera grips to best boys to producers and directors to movie distributors to your local theater.

The actors and actresses portraying your characters and speaking your words got paid because of you. Watch the credit crawl at the end of any movie. All of those people have jobs because a writer somewhere wrote a story.

And without you and other writers like you, those kids selling popcorn and tickets wouldn't have a place to work, either. But even that isn't all. Artists must design movie posters and cardboard standees for theaters, advertising agencies must create promotional campaigns.

With some movies, your subsidiary rights will also come into play, creating more jobs. Action figures and toy sets based on your characters require artists to design them, companies to produce them, outlets to sell them. Ditto branded T-shirts, coffee mugs, bumper stickers, and posters.

If you turn into another JK Rowling, you won't just be entertaining an audience, giving folks a nice break from their workaday lives while they read your book or watch the movie based on it or play with the toys created to support it.

You'll be a captain of industry, your very own publishing empire. You'll be creating the wealth of nations from the products of your mind and spreading this wealth out around the world.

But you don't have to be JK Rowling to make a difference. That's the magnificent thing about writing.

Even if right now you're just some kid working on your first novel in your bedroom, you're doing something good. You are creating something that didn't exist before, and that's wonderful. Beyond what it does for you, though, at barest minimum, you're supporting the economy as a consumer of pens and notebooks.

But if you dare to learn enough about the business to get good at it, you'll someday sleep well at night knowing that people all over the country, or maybe all over the world, are feeding their families and paying their bills in part because you had the guts to send your work out, and by doing so, to create money and jobs that would not have existed without you.

EXERCISE: Answer the following questions in between 100 and 250 words:

Who has already benefitted from the writing you've done, and how (include yourself in this answer)? Who will benefit if you keep writing — and *how* will they benefit?

Want to talk about this with other folks? Add your comment to the discussion on my weblog here:

http://hollylisle.com/discussion-on-money-from-nothing/

Writing With Integrity: Why Everyone SHOULDN'T Like You

I'd like to discuss *writing with integrity*.

Because you may not hear this today. You may not hear this in the next year. But sooner or later an editor or an agent or your mother or some dude at the supermarket checkout is going to tell you, "You need to change what you're writing to appeal to a broader audience."

You'll hear it from someone who wants to see you do well, who wants your numbers to go up (for her benefit as well as yours), or who thinks you could be doing better if you were writing work "like that vampire girl." Or, sadly, who doesn't respect what you write and wants to change you for your own good (as defined by him or her).

And depending on how much credence you give to the person saying this, you may be tempted to listen.

Be very, very careful. Before you change what you're writing in order to appeal to a broader audience, consider all the reasons why you may not want to. Here are the questions you ask yourself before you expend a gawdawful amount of time and energy doing something different so you can go haring off after people who don't like what you do right now.

Writing With Integrity Will Make — or Save — Your Career

Do you have an existing fan base?

Obviously, if no one is buying what you write, you can change anything and everything about your writing in the pursuit of readers.

But if you have readers who love what you do, you've created a connection. Your readers are real people who have found something that matters to them in your words, in the way you see the world, in the stories you tell and the characters you create and the situations you present.

If you have been writing true to yourself — writing with integrity — you have connected to people who think the way you do.

In a world where nobody seems to agree about anything, you've found people who understand how the world looks to you, and who share at least some of your view.

This is a rare and precious discovery. You don't throw the people who already love your work under the bus because someone else says you should.

Do you like what you write right now?

If you have no respect for the genre you're writing, the stories you're telling, the characters you create, or the view of the world you're presenting, yes, walk away. You probably got pulled into something because you thought you could make money at it, and failed to consider the price you'd pay for creating work you don't like. You aren't writing honestly — you're pretending to be someone you aren't, and nothing good comes of that.

But if your work comes from you, if your stories pull you out of bed in the middle of the night because you thought of one amazing line you have to get down before you lose it, if you fight right alongside your characters as you're writing them, desperate to know how they're going to move forward, you are living your work, and you are writing with integrity and creating something that matters.

Having been told that I needed to dumb down my work in one particular genre because I was writing too smart for my readers, I realized that I didn't want to write for readers who didn't want a complex, layered story. I'd been spoiled by my earliest fans, who were up to any challenge — and I decided *those* were the fans I wanted to keep.

I want the latitude to write complex, twisting plots and layered, complicated characters, and have that matter to my readers as much as it matters to me. I want to be free to NOT explain everything, and to know that my readers will look for the subtle clues I plant and get what's happening without having their hands held.

I love the stories I write…and those are the stories I *want* to keep writing. This joy in my work is what makes me keep coming back to it.

If you love what you're doing, evaluate what about it your would-be helpers want you to change, and decide whether you'll be as happy writing what they like as what *you* like.

Who likes you now, and who exactly are you trying to reach who doesn't like you now?

Take a moment to write down a description of your current reader. Age, interests, other authors he likes, type of work he does, what he likes most about the stories you tell. If you appeal to a cross-section of readers, figure out a discription of one person in each group. (These, by the way, are called avatars. There are all sorts of reasons for creating avatars, and figuring out where you want to take your writing career is a good one.) What areas of common ground do you share with each group? Why do you care about these people?

Now.

Do the same thing with the readers you think you would like to reach, but don't. Who are these people? What do **they** love, what interests them, where do they work, how do they play, and what do you have in common with them?

Why are you trying to reach them?

A lot of times, you'll discover that the only thing you have in common with groups you think you'd like to reach is that they spend money and you want them to spend some on what you've done.

This is what we call a *Bad Idea*. This doesn't mean it isn't a common idea. "I don't have to like it; I just have to get paid," is a form of prostitution. There is no writing integrity in following this path. You don't sleep with the book you hate for money, any more than you sleep with some scary dude with a wad of sweaty cash in his hand.

If you've identified more people you want to tell stories to, and you have some kick-ass stories to tell them that will matter to them, that's different. If you want to tell stories your current group of readers won't like, by all means expand. Write in both genres. If you have stories you simply can't tell unless you make changes, and you're dying to tell them, go for it.

But if you're pursuing people you don't respect for their money, don't think you're going to be the one Writer Whore who gets a happy ending.

And finally, why aren't the folks you're pursuing *already* reading your work?

If you're writing true to yourself (and I keep coming back to this because writing honestly is the most important job you have as a writer), the people who are reading you right now are going to be the right people for you. They get you, you matter to them, they matter to you. You folks deserve each other.

The people who don't like what you're doing aren't good enough for you. It isn't the other way around.

The people who are worth knowing are the ones who like you for who you are. They *become* worth knowing *because* they see the value in you and in what you do.

If you have to change who you are to win over people who don't like you, you're going to lose parts of yourself that matter. You're going to lose the people who liked what you did because you turned your back on values you and they shared. Writing with integrity is writing to the people who matter to you, about the subjects that matter to you.

If you look at your life and discover you need to make these changes to be the person you need to be, that's different. You do that, and you don't look back.

But don't change who you are for any reason except that you'll like yourself better in the morning if you do. In the end, your life will come down to whether you made yourself into someone you could admire and someone you could like — and *changing yourself and your work to please people who don't like you and don't like what you do is a guaranteed way to make sure your life will never be what you want it to be.*

EXERCISE: Answer the following question in between 100 and 250 words:

What do you love, and how can you make *that* what you write about?

Apples, Bananas: The Writer's Need for Experience

And now, a question. I throw you an object — roundish, reddish, with a short stem, a firm white flesh, seeds in the center, and you say "fruit" if you're being generic, or "apple" if you're being specific. I toss you another piece of fruit, this one yellow, maybe with a few brown spots, with a pulpy off-white flesh beneath a thick skin, and you say "banana." Here's the question.

What did you say wrong?

This is a discussion about life, and how the writer must see the world, and how the world conspires to blind the writer. And the first thing you must realize in this discussion is that the fruit I'm talking about is not a metaphor for anything. When I say apples and bananas, I am talking about…apples and bananas. The second thing you must bear in mind is that this matters, no matter how trivial it may seem.

Back to apples. You go into the grocery store most anywhere in the United States, most any time of the year. You can find apples. Red Delicious, Yellow Delicious, Granny Smith. Maybe Macintosh. They'll be in the produce section, well-waxed, beautiful to behold, stacked neatly in those geometric patterns grocers love. You take them home, you eat them, your brain says you ate an apple. But you didn't. You ate something with about as much taste as the wax fruit my grandmother used to keep on her table, and whatever that insipid thing was, it wasn't an apple.

Unless you live in the North and have access to the roadside produce stands or to growers' orchards, and you go out driving on one of those breathtaking autumn days when the sky has turned an impossible blue and the leaves on the sugar maples are crimson and maroon and lemon yellow, and unless you have purchased a small paper bag full of apples with names you have never heard before, you have never tasted an apple. You have tasted a lie, and been told it was an apple.

There are hundreds of varieties of apples, and there are apples that grow on abandoned farms in out-of-the-way back roads, apples almost too ugly to look at which have no names at all. When you bite into these apples, they are so sweet and tart and juicy and crisp that they bite you back, and your eyes water and their sharp, tangy scent burrows a hole into your brain and fixes there forever the taste of the apple and the rough texture of its imperfect skin and the color of the sky on the day you tasted it and the sound of water from the spring just above the roadside stand and the scent of growing grass and mouldering leaves and cold air touched with both the heartbreaking memory of summer gone and the promise of the coming of winter, and soaked overall in the unbearable beauty of the moment that vanishes before you can blink, but that will be with you always.

Real apples don't make it into the grocery stores. Only the apple-shaped frauds that are so durable that they can be waxed and preserved and fixed like bugs in formaldehyde and kept almost forever touch the lips of most people. Most people have never tasted an apple.

Have you?

Well, then, on to bananas. Bananas. What can anyone say about bananas? They aren't like apples. You can concede that the best apples don't travel well, that probably by the time they've sat in storage forever the market apples don't have much flavor … but a banana is a banana is a banana, right? You have Chiquita, you have Dole, and maybe one or two other kinds, and every banana you ever tasted has been pretty much like every other banana you ever tasted, and if there were ever a mediocre fruit, that fruit would be the banana. Bland, inoffensive, polite. Nice. A cornflakes-and-lunchboxes fruit.

And every banana you have ever tasted — if you get all your bananas from the grocery store — has been as much a lie as those pathetic excuses for apples you know so well. There are as many kinds of real bananas as there are real apples. Tiny bananas the size of your fingers that are so sweet and rich they make an ambrosial desert all by themselves, bananas long as your forearm that are bitter unless fried in strips and eaten hot and crunchy, bananas with reddish skins, bananas with firm flesh, bananas with bite. Coming soon to a grocery store near you?

Not likely. You can buy all these wonderful bananas in the open-air markets in Central America by bargaining with the old, dark-eyed woman who sits on the cobblestones next to the white-plastered, bullet-riddled ruins of the old Catholic church. They arrived in town that morning on the back of her burro, and next Saturday she will bring more. You will not see these bananas in Nebraska or Arkansas or New York because the good bananas, ripened by the sun and eaten immediately, have no way to get from that far-away place to your kitchen.

Unless the fruits you have come to think of as bananas are cut from the banana trees when they are hard and green and miles from ripe, they will rot in transit. And if they *are* cut from the tree while green, they will never have the flavor they would have had. And the exotic bananas look funny to the eyes of consumers, and wouldn't sell in sufficient numbers anyway. So if you get your bananas from a grocery store, you will never taste a real banana.

Apples.... Bananas ....

What else in your life has been lying to you? What other banal, insipid excuses have been masquerading as the real things, convincing you that you have lived and experienced the world when in fact you have been led around in blinders? If you are going where everyone else goes, and if you are doing what everyone else does, just about everything in your life has been a thin, weak broth, colored to look pretty and palatable, mass-produced to sell to a least-common-denominator clientele who are led into buying what isn't very good because they have been ignorant all their lives that better is out there.

Unless you have been to Alaska in the middle of the salmon run, when the black flies are biting like hell and the mosquitoes make blankets on every inch of exposed skin, and unless you have cut an inch-thick steak from a king salmon pulled fresh from the river and gutted right there, and unless you have wrapped that salmon steak in tin-foil filled with butter and perhaps pepper, and buried it in coals to cook, you have never tasted real salmon.

Have you ever walked across the tundra, feeling it give beneath your feet as if you were walking across a mattress that stretched as far as the eye could see — a mattress with shot springs and a coating of blueberries the size of your thumb and salmonberries and stands of fuscia fireweed that grow eye-high?

Have you ever ridden your bicycle along eastern Ohio's hilly back roads on a June day when the maples and the oaks shade the road and make the world look like a green cathedral, and the heat suppresses the sounds of everything but the drone of insects and the crunch of your tires on the gravel — when you stop and pick wild blackberries from the side of the road and get thorns in your thumb?

Have you ever pulled a live crayfish from under a slick, moss-coated rock in the chilly, clear stream where you are standing with your feet bare while your toes squoodge in the slick, sensuous mud — and the crayfish, cool and coarse-carapaced, waves claws and antennae at you and you admire the armor that covers his tail and the way his beady eyes watch you before you drop him in the water and he darts away backward?

What parts of your life are not homogenized, pasteurized, FDA-approved, plastic-wrapped, unscented, tasteless, pablum?

What have you seen that has not been filtered through the lying eye of television, or the movies — what have you heard that has not been influenced by radio, what have you read that is untouched and unsullied by corporations, the press, advertisers? What do you participate in that has no sponsor, no advertising, no board or council to promote it? What in your life is real?

And what does this have to do with writing?

Just this. *If you have never tasted a real apple, you will never write about an apple that is real.* If you have never felt an icy November rain soak through your clothes and drizzle down your spine and leave your nose cold and dripping and your eyes half-blind and blinking like defective windshield wipers, your characters will only be able to show readers the world from the inside of a heated automobile, or through the plate-glass window of a suburban house. If you have never lived, how are you going to write characters that live?

Real is free — or at least damned cheap. You want real?

Turn off the television, go outside, get away from people. Let your cheeks get chapped by the cold, burned by the sun.

Take a chance on that ugly fruit at the produce stand. Buy cloudy apple cider from your next-door neighbor who presses his own from the trees he grows in his back yard.

Walk or ride a bike. Smell the air around you — even if it stinks of sweat and exhaust from cars and trash from the dumpster at the corner, it's better for your writing than the recycled air-conditioned air you've been hiding in.

At least once, don't take anything when you get a headache. Let yourself hurt, and accept the hurt, and pay attention to it. At least once, cry when you're sad instead of pretending everything is fine.

At least once, give yourself something real to hold on to, because if all you know is sanitary plastic, all you will ever write is sanitary plastic.

EXERCISE: Answer the following question in between 100 and 250 words:

What have you experienced in your life that is real — not packaged, not processed, not made safe and tasteless and risk-free...and how can you use your experience in your writing?

One Good Enemy

Once upon a time, (back in 1985), I quit my nursing job to write a book. I was twenty-five years old, my husband made enough money that if we were careful we could pay bills and I could still stay home with both kids and work on the book, and I could have the chance I wanted to do what I wanted with my life. So I stayed home, and I wrote the book (it was a romance novel) and it was…well, it was, at best, mediocre, and then only if I wish to be kind to my fledgling effort. Actually, it was bad. I was looking at writing romances as my ticket to freedom because they seemed easy to write, not because they were what I loved beyond words. My lack of passion came through on the page, and when I sent the book out, it came back. Repeatedly.

I was crushed. I cried. I sank into a funk. I'd been so sure that all I had to do to make it as a writer was write, and publishers would buy what I wrote. Well, I was young and naïve, and I didn't yet realize that in order to sell what you do, in order to sell someone else on the words you've put on the page, you need to put your heart and your soul and perhaps even a pound of your flesh into them. You have to take your life and burn it onto the paper. At twenty-five, my experiences with life were still fairly limited, but even so, I could have done better than I did.

So.

Once upon a time, having quit a good Baylor weekend nursing job to spend a year writing a book, and having failed at the writing of said book, I had to go back to nursing with my tail tucked between my legs, while my husband and my family and his family all said, "Well, we didn't think it was going to work out anyhow, and we were right, and now you know you can't make it as a writer." And other equally encouraging things.

I worked the new nursing job. I wrote some short stories in my spare time (now science fiction, because I was beginning to understand that I needed to be working on stories I cared deeply about) but everything I wrote came back. Everything. Time passed.

In 1988, I managed to place a story ("Beneath the Wailing Wind") with a magazine that paid in copies (*Cosmic Landscapes*). The editor, Dan Petipas, wrote me an enthusiastic note, and I danced around in glee and told my husband and my family that I'd finally sold something.

The response was underwhelming.

I hadn't made a million dollars, and everyone told me the "sale" was nice but if no money exchanged hands, well...writing was really a waste of my time, wasn't it? From their perspective, it wasn't even a very good hobby, because at least with crocheting, you got a nice afghan for all the time you invested.

The story never made it into print. Dan changed the magazine format and I lost my computer copy, so "Beneath the Wailing Wind" died to the world. But in the meantime, I'd gotten in on the ground floor of a new SF/fantasy writers' group, and had become editor of the newsletter because I had more publishing experience than anyone else in the group. I did have that one acceptance letter, after all. And I had written a whole book, even if it sucked.

I kept writing. I kept not selling. My marriage, which had been a serious mistake, (I married a man whom I discovered much later was both a closet homosexual and a pedophile), hit the skids in a big way. I was still nursing. I was still writing. And suddenly I was looking for a way out of a private hell, and facing off against a determined enemy, who told me point-blank, "You've never been out on your own. You'll never make it without me."

Galvanizing words, those.

"You'll never make it without me."

My response, never voiced out loud, was, "Oh, yeah? Just watch me."

1989. I sold my guitar and my typewriter and a couple of other things to get together my first month's rent, and got myself a cheap place near where my soon-to-be-ex lived (because I had pushed for joint custody, and had gotten it. I did research when things were going to pieces and discovered that the only kids not terribly scarred by the divorce of their parents were those whose parents both remained equally involved in their lives. This statistic did not include children whose fathers turned out to be child molesters, but I didn't know anything about Barry's preferences yet. I just knew he didn't like me.) I worked my Baylor weekend nursing job to pay my bills, and I took care of my kids, and in my spare time I wrote.

God, I wrote like a fiend. Why?

Because of that smug smile, and that damnably calm little assertion — "You'll never make it without me." Because of the implication behind it — *you are nothing on your own*. Because I knew he wanted me to fail; because I knew that he, with his country club membership and Jaycees activities and the vice-presidency of his father's business, saw himself as a success; because I knew he took great pleasure in the fact that I lived in a tiny apartment with cardboard boxes for furniture.

1991. I wrote, and the book I wrote was *Fire in the Mist*. You'll have heard of that one if you've read my work. It was my first published novel. I sent it out, and the first publishing house I sent it to called me back a month later to buy it. One month from mail to sale. A bit of magic I never expected, though I did dare to hope. Aside from two sonnets that I sold to *Aboriginal*, ($25 apiece), it was my first real sale. My first validation. My first proof (aside from the nursing job) that I could make my dreams into reality.

Why did *Fire in the Mist* sell?

Because I wrote my heart and my life and my anger into it; because I transmuted my pain into story; because I was battling against an enemy and my blood boiled and I raged inside and I was determined that I *would ... not ... fail*. I swore that I could not fail — that no matter how long it took, no matter how hard I had to drive myself, I would show him that I could make it without him. He would eat his words.

And he ate his words. I sold enough books to go full-time. My books showed up with great regularity in the local bookstores. People mentioned them to him. I became known in town as a Real Writer. I was a guest at conventions and conferences; I was nominated for and sometimes won awards; all of this showed up in the local newspaper, alongside pictures of smiling me. I knew that knife twisted, and I took pleasure in the knowledge.

This isn't an enlightening, warm-fuzzies sort of story. This is, instead, a tale of revenge won with no weapon but a computer and a brain; a tale of anger and hurt and disillusionment transmuted into gold; a story, finally, of growing beyond the need for revenge. Finally, years later, I could look beyond showing him that I could make it without him. Finally, I could walk away from twisting the knife, and take pleasure in my accomplishments because they were mine, and because I loved my work. Finally I buried the ghost of "You'll never make it without me."

But that came later. Much later. And without the drive I got from needing my revenge; I don't know that it would have come at all. I might have stayed with my nursing job, unhappy because I wanted something different, dreaming of writing without ever making it happen. I might have felt the desire without ever fulfilling it; I might have longed and yearned and done nothing. Failing that first time left its scars. I can still, after all these years, close my eyes and feel the humiliation and the shame of thinking I could win, and losing so publicly. Fear of feeling that humiliation again could have kept me in a cage of my own creation for the rest of my life. Without the push of "You'll never make it without me," I might have succumbed to the fear, and in so doing failed myself.

Now.

Here is where this grim little tale reaches out and touches you. When you're complaining that you aren't getting enough support for your writing; when you're down because everything you write is coming back; when you aren't burning when you put the words on the page and the stories you tell come only from your head, and not from your soul; when you are praying that things will get easier ... maybe you need to stop and consider the possibility that you're praying for the wrong thing. Maybe you don't need a friend to tell you what you want to hear, to cheer you up, to make you feel good about yourself. Maybe you don't need positive feedback, warm fuzzies, understanding and compassion, people who will believe in you.

Maybe what you should be praying for is one good enemy.

EXERCISE: Answer the following question in between 100 and 250 words:

Who is the one person in your life, past or present, you would love to prove was wrong about you — and how can you take the emotions you still feel about that person and turn those emotions into the drive that will keep you writing when things are hard?

How to Tell Who WON'T Make It in Writing (and How Not to Be That Writer)

I've met thousands of unpublished writers since I started selling my work. I've corresponded with at least several thousand more. I've heard every possible hope and dream about writing, commiserated with sad tales of rejection, cheered over jubilant good news, and listened to more plots than the FBI and more dirt than the parish priest sitting in his confessional.

And I've discovered something important. I couldn't in a million years tell you who among those thousands of hopeful writers will eventually succeed. But I can tell you in about five minutes which writers are guaranteed to fail.

The guaranteed failures among writerdom carry their amateur beliefs and attitudes and methods like a bad perfume — an ever-present cloud of Eau de Doom that rolls off of their bodies and wafts into the noses of publishers and editors and readers who might otherwise be interested in the writer's work, sending the pros fleeing to green rooms and bathrooms to escape and readers fleeing to writers who DO value professionalism.

If you're wearing this particular scent, you need to lose it. Fast. Read below for a quick sniff-test, and for the best ways to come clean.

The Writer's Stench O' Doom Checklist

The Big But

I'm a very good listener, I'm patient, and I'm interested in seeing beginning writers succeed. In consequence, I spend much of my time at conventions and writers' conferences leaned up against a convenient wall or doorframe, listening to the dreams and aspirations and tales of woe and book descriptions of unpublished or rarely published writers. These writers usually want a listener more than anything, so mostly I just listen. But from time to time, a hopeful writer will ask my advice. I always take my time, give the question my full attention, and try to offer the best answer I can, based on my experience and what I know of the markets and the industry.

About two thirds of the time, my questioner's immediate response starts off with, "But I can't do that because...."

At which point, I'm out of the conversation. I'm starting to look for a quick exit and just about any exit will do. It isn't that I think my advice would turn this writer into an overnight success, or even necessarily get his or her manuscript looked at; it isn't that the writer has hurt my feelings by ignoring me (you don't get this far in the business without developing a pretty tough hide).

The problem with people who say "But...." is that they have already decided they know everything they need to know about writing. They may be chatting me up in the hopes of networking, or because they want me to tell them that theirs is the most brilliant idea I've ever heard. But they aren't interested in getting published. And they aren't going to get published.

Of all the possible sins the hopeful writer can commit, The Big But is the worst. **You cannot make excuses for your writing and hope to succeed.**

If someone who knows the industry tells you that your manuscript isn't right for Knopf and you need to submit to other markets, don't say, "But I only want it to be published by Knopf."

If a pro tells you that your plot is hackneyed and your characters are thin, "But I intended it to be that way...." is decidedly the wrong answer.

If an editor tells you that you're going to have to give the story a real ending, "But I want to leave the reader in suspense...." is going to get you round-filed and lose you a big opportunity.

Here are some of the amazing excuses I've heard.

"But the editor can clean up the spelling and the grammar."

(It'll never happen. He'll just get tons of form rejections.)

"But I don't want to write a second book until the first one sells."

(This person isn't a writer. This person is someone who wants to have a published book on the shelf so she can call herself a writer.)

"But the first book is the start of a twelve-book series — the editor has to buy that one first."

(Not necessarily. The editor can buy someone else's book. If book one isn't selling anywhere, write something different. Something that stands alone, maybe.)

"But if there isn't sex in every chapter, no one will read the damned thing."

(Untrue. Lots of novels that hit the bestseller lists have no sex in them whatsoever. Does tell you something about what this writer *reads*, though.)

"But I want it to be hard to read — I want to sell my books to intelligent readers."

(Seriously? *Seriously, dude?* There is a difference between "written to a college reading level" and "rambling, obtuse, good-God-were-you-high-when-you-wrote-this?" and the polite professional writer telling him he has written the second sort of manuscript does so with the words, "You need to make this clearer and easier to read.")

"But it doesn't need to have a plot — it's literary."

(This may, in fact, be true — but since the book hadn't sold, I'm willing to bet that in at least this instance, even the editor of literary books would have welcomed a story that seemed to be going somewhere.)

"But I'm a published writer now; I shouldn't have to revise."

(A moment of stunned silence followed by a laugh of sheer, shocked disbelief follows. She honest-to-Pete said that. She had sold one book many years earlier and had failed to sell anything else. Wanna take a guess why?)

One more time, then. **You cannot make excuses for your writing and hope to succeed.**

Open Mouth — Closed Ears

They sit in the front row of each writing panel at a convention with their arms crossed over their chests, smug smiles on their faces. They know all the answers, and they talk over not just the other attendees, but also the panelists. They corner the pros in the hallways after the panel is over and launch into long spiels about their future publishing career.

Their entire goal in attending conventions, conferences, and seminars is to prove to the writers, editors and publishers there that they know as much about the field as the pros — that they have done their homework — that they are a part of the inner circle.

The problem is that they never shut up long enough to listen to anyone, and as a result they miss the important information they could have gained, and kill the good-will they could have won. Yes, they are smart people; I've been talked at by a bunch of 'em. I've been amazed by their erudition — but appalled by their ruthless head-on charges and their utter obliviousness to the fact that the very people they hope to impress are gnawing off the arm they're clutching at the wrist in order to get away from them.

So, if you recognize yourself as being the adult version of the kid in class with his hand always up going "Me, me, me," here are a couple of tips.

Life is not school.

There is no test.

You don't get an "A" for shouting out the answers.

Nobody cares how smart you are — they care how willing you are to treat them like equals.

The art of conversation does not consist of thinking of the next witty thing you're going to say while waiting for the other person to breathe so you can jump in and say it. It consists of actually listening and responding.

If you cannot learn to listen, you will not succeed.

Sacred Writ-ism

The third leg of the Holy Trinity of Doom Signs is the phrase "I don't believe in revision."

Robert Heinlein offered some wonderful advice to writers, and created some brilliant books and some unforgettable characters, but he also offered this one piece of advice that simply leaves me open-mouthed with disbelief. He said, in his list of rules for writers, "Rule Three: You Must Refrain From Rewriting, Except to Editorial Order."

This is a great rule if you're already writing publishable prose. But I've had this rule quoted back to me with a sanctimonious little sniff by people whose sentences didn't parse, whose grammar indicated that the story had been written in one language and translated into a second by someone who only spoke a third and unrelated tongue, whose characters were dead on page one and who wouldn't have known a plot if one reached up out of the open grave of their manuscripts and strangled them to get their attention.

If you are not writing professionally publishable prose, the only thing that will get you an editorial order for revision is a whole lot of un-ordered revision while you learn what you're doing. And the best way to find out if you're writing professionally publishable prose is to ask yourself this one easy question. "Have I ever had a professional editor (or reputable agent) send me a personal response, telling me that if I fixed something specific in my story, he would buy it (or represent me)?"

If the answer to that question is "no," you have two choices. You can assume that your work does not yet meet professional standards, or else you can hope that it simply has not yet found its market.

And the variant here for self-publishers is, "Are my books selling steadily and do the people who read them leave mostly positive ratings, and buy my next book when it comes out?" If the answer to those three questions (sales, ratings, and repeat readers) is "no," you have the same two choices.

While it would be nice to believe the second, repeated submissions will either confirm this for you (someone will buy it or tell you it's great and with a few changes, she'll buy it) or deny it in pretty short order. If you never get any feedback that indicates that you're close, assume that the work is not yet of professional caliber and get busy revising.

If you assume that the words that flow from your fingertips were dictated to you by God and are thus sacred and immune from revision, only you and God are ever going to read them.

Now here's the good news. No perfume — not even Eau de Doom — sticks forever if you wash it off. Even if you've been making excuses, failing to listen, and believing that revision was evil, you can leave your doomed past behind. You can sell your work. Go to it.

EXERCISE: Answer the following question in between 100 and 250 words:

What bad attitudes, bad beliefs, or bad habits do you have that could hold you back from making writing your career — and what can you do right now to fix them?

QUIZ: Are You Right for Writing?

You're pretty sure you can string together sentences in a coherent manner. You even have fun doing it. And God knows you'd love to see your name on the cover of a book — maybe a best-seller, even.

But do you have what it takes to be a writer, year in and year out? Could you write your way into a decent supplemental income? Could you write your way out of your day job?

I can't promise you a definite answer, but I might be able to give you a pretty good idea. Take my *Are You Right for Writing* quiz and find out where you rank on the writing personality index.

This is not a scientific tool; it is simply the product of my years of observing myself and my colleagues and trying to figure out what makes the whole herd of us tick. I'm a good observer, though; I'd trust the results of my quiz over any you might find in **Cosmo**.

Okay. Just answer honestly. If you start this out by lying to yourself, skip writing and go straight into politics. The money is better and you'll be a lot happier.

Question 1:

You've turned off the TV, the stereo, and every other possible entertainment device, you have removed all books, and you are sitting in a dimly-lit room doing absolutely nothing. So...how long can you sit without going crazy?

- A. 5 seconds. I get cold sweats just thinking about power outages.

- B. 15 minutes — but only if I have a bag of potato chips.

- C. 1 hour — I can always replay my last argument and come up with wittier things I could have said.

- D. Man! I lost track of the time. I started watching people in my imagination doing interesting things, and the next thing I knew, it was nighttime and I'd missed supper.

Question 2:

You're writing and the phone rings. You:

- A. Answer it.

- B. Finish your sentence, then answer it.

- C. Let the answering machine get it.

- D. Have no phone access in the room where you work.

Question 3:

The person calling is one of your dearest friends, who wants to get together for brunch and a good long chat about his/her ex. Unfortunately, this juicy brunch will take place during your peak writing time. You:

- A. Decide to go. You haven't heard the latest dirt on the evil ex in ages.

- B. Reschedule for a later hour.

- C. Reschedule for a non-writing day.

- D. Pass.

Question 4:

You're out at the restaurant with your friend when you have a fantastic idea for a novel. You:

- A. Have to hope you'll remember it — you have nothing to write with and nothing to write on.

- B. Will manage. You always have a pen, and there are napkins in restaurants.

- C. Carry a special notebook, an organizer, or even a laptop with you everywhere — you're completely prepared.

- D. Aren't at the restaurant; that would cut unacceptably into your 14-hour writing workday.

Question 5:

When you see yourself as a successful writer, what is the image that is clearest in your mind:

- A. The rounds of publishers' parties, autographings, and talk shows where you are lionized for your work of immortal literary genius?

- B. Your name on the spines of a shelf full of beautiful books?

- C. A vision of sending off a completed manuscript to a waiting editor or agent?

- D. Your butt in your chair, your fingers on your keyboard, and your eyes on your monitor (or whatever tools you use to produce your stories or novels.)

Question 6:

You anticipate being able to quit your day job to write full time:

- A. immediately — you have a great idea for a book you know will be a bestseller;

- B. as soon as the first book sells;

- C. when you have three or four on the shelf;

- D. when you're making as much from writing as you make at your day job...and have done so for a couple of years.

Question 7:

Do you have. . .

- A. an idea for the Great American Novel — a certain best-seller;
- B. a few ideas for different stories;
- C. background and development for a number of related books, a timeline, and a whole handful of novel ideas;
- D. half a dozen fully developed worlds, including maps, costume worksheets, fully developed languages, cultures, flora, fauna, religions, sciences, and much more, plus enough story ideas to get you through this lifetime, and the next one.

Question 8:

You figure the biggest benefit of becoming a writer is:

- A. Money & fame;
- B. Flexible hours;
- C. Creative control and being your own boss;
- D. The writing.

Question 9:

You read:

- A. The occasional newspaper, magazines, and remember having read books...but not recently;
- B. You read in your free time if you don't have something better to do;

- C. You invented the term multi-tasking because reading IS your "something better to do" — you usually have a book in hand no matter what else you're doing at the time;

- D. Your house doesn't need insulation; the triple-stacked shelves of all your books will serve quite nicely, thank you. *(The electronic corollary to this is that you already own most of the ebooks on the internet, and have to write now just to have something new to read.)*

Question 10:

Where is the weirdest place you have ever written?

- A. Your desk...*maybe*, in a crunch, at the kitchen table;

- B. In bed. (An extra 10 points for this one if you were on your honeymoon at the time);

- C. On the toilet;

- D. Don't ask.

Scoring the Quiz

Give yourself 1 point for each A answer you gave, 3 points for each B answer, 6 points for each C answer, and 10 points for each D answer. Add up your answers, then check out the short key below before going on to the discussion.

10 — 29 points — You have some seriously romanticized ideas of what writing for a living is like. You're going to be badly disappointed by the reality.

30 — 49 points — There's hope; you suspect some of the darker truths about the profession, and have an idea of what some of the rewards are. If you really want to do this, you'll face some disillusionment, but also stand a good chance of finding the real joys of the profession.

50 — 79 points — If you can write, you're in there.

80 — 103 points — You'll probably make a great writer. You should think very carefully before getting married, having children, or buying a pet, however. Walking into your living room and discovering the dust-covered skeleton that was your cat — or your spouse — can be really bad for morale.

And Now The Discussion

Quizzes have always seemed worthless to me if they didn't include a discussion of why any given answer was good or bad. So my quiz includes a question-by-question discussion.

Question 1 Answers — That empty room with nothing going on was not a hypothetical situation. That's the writer's work day. You, a quiet room, and nothing happening except for what's going on between your ears. This is pretty much a make-or-break question: if you can't entertain yourself for at least a few hours a day with no source of entertainment but your thoughts, you're not going to have much fun writing for a living.

Question 2 Answers — As long as you have no one depending on you, D is the ideal answer — but most of us live in a world where *someone* we love might, at some point, need us. So we don't have the option of seclusion. The self-control of screening out all but emergency calls with an answering machine (or looking for the name of the person calling on your cellphone before answering, and only answering calls from your priority people during work hours) becomes the real-world, practical answer.

Question 3 Answers — This one depends on how much you want to hang onto your friends, but also on how often such invitations come. The friend who routinely disrupts your writing time (if he *knows* it's your writing time — making sure he knows when you write is up to you) isn't much of a friend.

However, if you're passing on spending time with someone who is usually respectful of your schedule but who could use some support now, *you* aren't much of a friend. Writing needs to hold an important place in your life, but if you plan on having a life, it can't hold the number one spot.

Question 4 Answers — I come in with a solid C on this one: because I always (yes, always) have my Visor with me, I could actually write the book on the spot, were I so inclined. *(Okay, so now it's my iPhone. Same concept, better software.)* You need to keep some tools with you all the time. Visor, tape recorder, or even just a little notepad and a pen — you need to have something to record great lines, bits of dialogue, or character or story ideas while you're out. And you can't count on everyone to have napkins you can borrow.

Question 5 Answers — If you chose answer A for this question, sit down. I have bad news. No one is going to hold a ticker tape parade in your honor because you wrote a book, or even a bunch of books. Aside from your spouse, your agent, and your eventual fans, no one *CARES* that you're a writer. You won't be recognized in restaurants and hounded for your autograph. Hell, you won't even be recognized in bookstores unless you introduce yourself. And maybe not even then.

If your answer was B, you're getting warmer. The name-on-the-books thing is big. But you're looking for happiness a long way from its source. In almost all cases, it takes a minimum of about two years from the time you start writing the book until the time it sees print. That's best case, when you have a contract for the book. If you have to write the book and then sell it, you could be in for a very long haul.

If you chose answer C, mailing off a finished manuscript, you're edging close to home, but not there yet. If you're very prolific, you'll complete two or three first-draft novels in a year. I usually do one or two. I have friends and colleagues who do a book every two years or less. That's a long time to wait for the thrill.

If you picked D, you have the best chance of being happy enough with what you're doing to do it long enough to succeed. To be a career writer, you really ought to like to write. You ought to have fun sitting in your little corner of the kitchen or your office, if you're lucky enough to have one, coming up with neat stuff to do to your characters. If you can learn to get your joy from that, you can be happy nearly every day.

Question 6 Answers — I know the temptation to quit the day job. Boy, do I. As someone who once dumped a *really* good straight-days weekend-Baylor nursing job on the strength of just an idea — and then had to go get a job that was less good a year later when things didn't pan out, I'm aware of just how strong that pull can be. And what a mistake it can be to give in to it.

If you're desperate to get out of your day job, you're probably not going to listen to me, but I'll say this anyway; the longer you hold on to your day job after you start selling your work (and the smarter you are about hanging on to the writing money), the less likely you'll be to give up on writing in desperation a year or several years down the road, when the grind of never knowing when — or if — you're going to get paid drags you under.

Question 7 Answers — An idea for one book is a good start, but except in the rarest of cases, one book does not make a career. If you are already giving some thought to what you're going to do for an encore, and for the encore after that, you're thinking like a pro.

Question 8 Answers — If you think the main benefit of being a writer is money and fame, think again. When most first novels sell for around $5000 to $7500 dollars (and this is for something that may have taken years to write), and most novels disappear from shelves in weeks, never to be seen again, and most readers cannot tell you the names of the authors of most of the books they liked, much less recognize those authors by sight, your chance at finding great wealth or public adulation in this business is vanishingly small.

And the dark truth about most self-pubbed novels is that while you can put them together for damn near free if you're not including the value of your own time in your math (and you should be), most self-pubbed novels sell as badly as or worse than most commercially published novels. And this won't change, simply because of Sturgeon's Law: 90% of everything is crap.

http://en.wikipedia.org/wiki/Sturgeon%27s_Law

As for flexible hours...yes, they are flexible. When I was getting started as a pro, they flexed from the minute the kids left for school in the morning until they got home in the afternoon, and then from 9 p.m., after they went to bed, until I couldn't force my eyes open any longer, every day off. Since I worked 12 hour weekend nursing shifts and had older children, I at least had long blocks of time to write. Before the kids started school, it was a lot harder to find time.

As for taking days off — you can take off any day you want. You just don't get paid. I've had one vacation since 1991, when I sold the first book. I don't work 10-hour days anymore, which is nice. I do work seven days a week most weeks. And I never have enough time to do everything I want. **Rule of thumb for the self-employed:** *It's illegal for anyone to ask you to work as long or as hard as you'll be working for yourself.*

Creative control is great. No caveats there. Being your own boss is great, too — except that your boss is probably going to have to be a slave-driver if you're going to make it professionally.

If your reward is the writing, though, even the long hours, the poor or nonexistent pay, and the anonymity will be no big deal.

Question 9 Answers — I've never known a successful writer who wasn't also a compulsive reader. The only real difference between the third answer to this question and the fourth is that some of us are book packrats, and some of us aren't. But if you aren't a big reader, you're going to have a terrible time figuring out what is a truly different approach to a story and what has been done to death.

Question 10 Answers — You may be asking, "What could it possibly matter where I've written, or under what circumstances?"

Writing at odd times and in unlikely places simply serves as a clear sign of how deeply the writing bug has bitten you. Case in point — I'm writing this right now on the backlit screen of my Visor, sitting on the floor in the middle of a neighborhood blackout, hanging out with my family. And writing. This isn't the weirdest place, or the weirdest situation, in which I have written. I definitely earn a D "you don't want to know" response to this question.

The presence of that unstoppable — sometime unbearable — urge to put words on a page is a good sign that you have a chance of outlasting the early-career hard times. If you can stay writing long enough to learn your craft, and still be hungry for the next word after years of next words, you just might make it.

I'll leave you with one of my favorite quotes about writers by a writer:

"I could claim any number of highflown reasons for writing, just as you can explain certain dog behavior as submission to the alpha, or even as a moral choice. But maybe it's that they're dogs, and that's what dogs do."

Amy Hempel

EXERCISE: Answer the following questions in between 100 and 250 words:

What was your score, and is there anything about yourself you can change to improve it? And do you really want to?

SECTION II
Practice: The Workshops

In the workshops, you won't have questions to answer. Instead, you'll have **Your Turn**, where you'll read the workshop, then create some new writing of your own, trying out each technique in turn. You can download the free worksheets for this section here:

http://howtothinksideways.com/mugging-the-muse

If you don't already have an account on the site, you'll need to create one. Site accounts are also free. Use the links on the page above to login to your account or create one.

If you run past the worksheet and are still writing, get out your writing notebook and keep going.

Follow your idea, and chase whatever wonderful story or character or bit of dialogue you come up with from the exercise as far as it will take you.

Mostly, have fun exploring.

Creating Conflict, or The Joys of Boiling Oil

You're sitting at your desk staring at your manuscript, realizing that you've written ten or fifty or three hundred (ouch) pages in which nothing really happens. People talk to each other and they go places and they do things, but you couldn't find enough suspense in what they're doing to fill a thimble, and you're creeping up on the sneaking suspicion that your book is a wash, your ideas were stupid, and your characters are duds. Or worse, that you are. Maybe it's time to throw in the towel, admit defeat, take your parents' advice and go into the family wax-dummy business.

Don't do that. **You can fix this.** It may not be easy, but if you want to save your characters and your idea and at least some of the work you've already done, you can.

You're going to need to dig a bit. But, hell, if you don't, you're looking at a long future of gluing fake eyebrows on bee byproduct. You have a compelling reason to succeed at this, right? You'll do pretty much anything to avoid the future everybody else planned out for you? Just like they'd do just about anything to have you follow in your father's footsteps and be the next Wax King or Wax Queen.

Yeah.

Well, that's conflict.

You have it in real life. You have something that you want enough that you're willing to suffer for it, work for no pay to get it, endure the slings and arrows of outrageous disbelief and mockery if you can just have it. And on the other side of the fence, the person who is doing the arrow-slinging has equally compelling reasons for standing in your way.

Now you just have figure out how to move conflict from your life to the page.

There are three types of conflict, and you deal with all three every day, and so should every one of your characters.

Get out your notebook, or open up a new document, or grab your quill and parchment. We're going to do some quick-and-dirty conflict-building.

Meet Bob

Bob Vanilla is twenty-five, he has held a few jobs in his life but nothing that ever thrilled him, he's had a couple of girlfriends, but no one who ever thrilled him, and he has a brother named Jim and a sister named Jane. If ever the Muse tossed out a character born to lie dead on a page, 'twas Bob.

Your job is to fix his life — fiction-writer style. Which means you dip him in batter, dump him in boiling oil, and don't take him out until he's brown and tasty. You're going to mess with his mind, trash his relationships, and top it all off by dropping a comet on his head.

For the Wee Gods of Storytelling declare — THOU SHALT HAVE CONFLICT ON EVERY PAGE.

And if thou wants to sell thy damned story, thou wiltst.

Creating Internal Conflict

(Bob against Bob)

Bob wants something. A lot. He wants something so much that he would do almost anything to get it. What does he want?

Maybe he wants to be a championship surfer, riding the waves in Hawaii and bringing home the big-bucks endorsement deals from… uh… Nike Surf or Toe Jam Board Wax.

But Bob is going to have trouble getting want he wants because something inside of him stands in his way.

Maybe Bob is afraid of something. Maybe a sister that you never met, Janet, got eaten by a shark. Maybe Bob almost drowned in a bathtub when he was seventeen, and now he's terrified of more than three gallons of water in any one place.

Or maybe not.

Maybe Bob wants love and passion and a lot of hot sex at least once a week. And is secretly in love with a girl who is beautiful, and kind, and funny, and stacked like a triple-decker beef burger, and who is witty and virtuous but not too virtuous.

And maybe Bob looks like a flounder, and has half the self-confidence.

Maybe he hates his dull life and has always dreamed of becoming an Army Ranger, only he's weak and skinny and just about to become too old to enlist, and he's afraid of the dark, and of snakes, and of being shot at, and he doesn't know if he has what it takes to be a hero. He thinks he might just be a jellyfish.

Whatever he wants, it's the biggest thing in the world to him, the one thing that could, if he got it, drag him out of bed in the wee hours of the morning and keep him up all night. And the first thing that stands in his way is himself.

Your turn.

Write down five different things that YOUR Bob might want with a passion. Write down five different internal conflicts that stand in the way of his getting what he wants (one for each desire.)

Creating Interpersonal Conflict

(Bob against Someone Else)

Okay. You've messed with Bob's head. Good. Hope you made it tough in there for him. Now you're going to cause him problems with the people around him.

Because Bob wants something. A lot. And people around him don't want him to get what he wants.

I'll take Bob and the Army as my working conflict. Bob wants to do something that matters with his life. He wants to go to work every day knowing that he's contributing to something that's bigger than he is; he wants the sense of mission and purpose that a job as a Ranger would give him.

His mother wants him to be safe and stay way the hell out of harm's way.

His father wants him to take over Vanillaville Mini-Widgets and spend the rest of his life making light switches and those little rubber things that cover telephone number-pad keys. (You're not the only one facing a grim future in the family business.)

His current girlfriend, Jill, wants him. She is head-over-heels in love with him (and the nice lifestyle that a VP in Vanillaville Mini-Widgets could give her). She wants him to marry her and settle down in Vanillaville so that her mother can come over and visit every day. Jill also wants fourteen kids, and is determined to get them. From Bob.

And his best friend since kindergarten, Jeff, wants Bob to stay put, because if Bob goes out and does something big and important with his life, Jeff is going to be left at home playing poker and drinking beer alone — and the dullness of Vanillaville is going to become very sharp and clear to him.

So...

- Bob's mother may cry and fake fainting spells and check herself into the hospital to convince Bob not to go

- Bob's father may lie to the recruiter and tell him Bob has a criminal record

- Bob's girlfriend may poke holes in Bob's condoms

- Bob's best friend may clip out every article of Army Rangers getting hurt or killed in action that he can find

These are the things the people who *love* him are doing to keep him from getting what he wants. Imagine what the guy who can't stand him will do.

Your turn.

Write down five people who want YOUR Bob **not** to get what he wants, exactly what each of them wants (and why), and what each of them will do to stand in Bob's way.

Creating External Conflict

(Bob [and perhaps others] against
Something BIG)

But you aren't done with poor ol' Bob. Hell hath no fury like a writer on a roll, and now, with internal and interpersonal conflicts all brewing at the same time (because Bob didn't suddenly get big and strong and grow a stainless steel backbone when his mother faked the heart attack, after all), you're going to drop one more conflict on his head. The biggie.

Aliens from Bugeyed IV might drop in on Vanillaville and the rest of the country for a little snack.

Terrorists might kidnap Bob's girlfriend and hold her hostage.

A comet might aim itself right at Vanillaville.

An earthquake, a tornado, a torch-carrying mob from Cinnamontown bent on the destruction of its arch-rival, food-shortages, plague, drought, a million dollars missing from the Library Fund tip jar. You need something that Bob can't ignore — and that no one else with any sense can, either. Something big. Something powerful. Something that will push Bob to be the hero he wants to be, but is afraid to be. That will give him reasons to win people to his side, that will cause him to make powerful enemies, that will change him and everyone around him forever.

In a story with smaller scope, the external conflict can be the IRS taking the hero's mom and dad's house for back taxes, or the school burning down, or the appearance of the rare Yellow-Backed Purple-Butted Bark Chewer in woods that haven't seen one for a century. To the right hero, even that sort of thing could change his world forever.

Your turn.

Hurt YOUR Bob. Hit him with something on the outside that smacks him upside the head with a fifty-pound rubber mallet and that says to him, **Go. Go now. Do. Be. Or the dream you hold dear, and everything that hangs on it, will die.**

One external conflict, and what he's going to do about it. And who is going to help him, and who is going to oppose him, and how he's going to overcome his own fears and handicaps, and ….

And there's your book. Or your story. Focus on what Bob wants, what his people want, and what the universe intends to do to him, give him obstacles worth struggling over and let him struggle with everything in him, losing some and winning some, and you'll never spend another day trying to tug vinyl pants over melting wax legs again.

Scene Creation Workshop: Writing Scenes that Move Your Story Forward

As the atom is the smallest discrete unit of matter, so the scene is the smallest discrete unit in fiction; it is the smallest bit of fiction that contains the essential elements of story. You don't build a story or a book of words and sentences and paragraphs — you build it of scenes, one piled on top of the next, each changing something that came before, all of them moving the story inexorably and relentlessly forward.

You can, of course, break the scene up into its component pieces — words, sentences, and paragraphs — but only the scene contains the vital wholeness that makes it, like an atom of gold, a building block of your fiction. It contains the single element that gives your story life, movement, and excitement. Without this one element, you don't have a scene, you merely have a vignette.

So what is this magical element that gives your scene its life and makes it the brick with which you build your fiction?

Change.

When is a scene a scene? When something changes. What defines the completion of a scene? The moment of change.

We're going to create some very short scenes here — I'll do some demos, and then you'll do some practice scenes. We'll start with the simplest of all possible scenes and work our way to scenes of greater complexity. But you'll find out that even the most complex of scenes become rather simple when taken down to its component parts.

Let's start with the most basic of basic scenes. One setting, no characters, a single elemental change. I'll do one, and then you'll do one. Here we go:

In the heart of the command center, a single wire, stiff and brittle from ten-thousand cycles of heating and cooling, snapped away from its circuit board. The break set off an alarm — a tiny pulse of electricity that raced through the wires to a monitored board at a control panel half a mile away. The pulse reached its destination, a tiny light that should have come to brilliant red life. But the light — never used, infrequently tested — failed to switch on.

Those two tiny failures — broken circuit; burned-out bulb — would have unimaginable consequences.

Okay. That's a whole scene, though there isn't much to it. It comprises the essential elements of scene — a place, a time frame, and a change that moves the story forward. We know that something vitally important has happened, because we're reading about it. (If it weren't important, why write it?) We have some feel for the story — lives no doubt will depend upon the smooth functioning of the control panel and the command center, and we already know that there's a glitch that no one else knows about. When we started into the scene, the command center was working smoothly. When we left it, there was a problem, and a problem heightened by the fact that the people who needed to know about it didn't.

Your Turn

Write a brief scene with no characters, a clear location, a limited period of time, and a single event that changes and moves the story forward. (You don't actually have to have a story in mind. Just pretend you do.) When you've finished it, come back and we'll move on.

Okay. Next, we'll do something a bit fancier. This time, we'll do a scene that has one character in it. No dialogue yet. No interaction. Just one person making one change. Here's mine.

He danced into the kitchen through the green double doors. He swirled. He pirouetted. He wore her blue dress, her blonde wig — the Dolly Parton one — her bra (and stuffed into her bra several pairs of his own dark blue lightweight wool dress socks), and her Elizabeth Arden makeup, which he had applied with a skill that would have astonished her.

He tangoed past the refrigerator, humming something dramatic from the opera they'd attended the night before — he didn't know the name of the piece, but had not been able to get it out of his head since he'd heard it. He slid between the blue-tiled counter and the butcher block island on which sat bright red bowls full of peaches and lemons and oranges. He gave his hips an electric shimmy, admired his reflection in the floor-to-ceiling mirrors that covered the kitchen's far wall, and reached his arms left — right — left. On the second left, something flashed in the morning sunlight, then disappeared into the blue dress's deep pocket.

He spun, kicking up a leg with a grace that would have shamed many a chorus girl, and tangoed back out the way he had come, still humming.

On the kitchen counter, a single empty slot in the knife block marked his passage. Top right slot — one of the big ones. Instead of fourteen knives, there were now unlucky thirteen.

The heels of his dancing shoes clattered up the elegant oak staircase — size thirteen shoes, black patent, with three-inch heels suitable for dancing. He'd looked a long time before he found those shoes.

What changes occur here? Our expectations of the character are the primary change. We find out at the beginning that he's at least a cross-dresser, and (as suggested by his skill with makeup) one who's been hiding his secret for a while. We discover that he's either married or living with a woman; we know that she has expensive taste in makeup and questionable taste in wigs; we know that she doesn't know about his hobby.

Initially he seems harmless and happy, if a bit weird — but as the scene goes on, we get a tiny surge of foreboding (lightly foreshadowed by the **butcher** block, the red of the bowls) with the mysterious something that flashes in the morning light before disappearing into the pocket of the dress.

With the revelation that the knife block is suddenly one knife short (the slot in the top right is usually reserved for the butcher knife, incidentally), our friend's antics no longer seem so harmlessly eccentric. And the revelation that he bought the shoes himself — that he spent a great deal of time finding just the right ones, suggests a change in his habits, an intensification or commitment to something going on inside of him that, tied in with the missing knife, bodes badly for the future.

Your Turn

Write a scene in which a single character moves through one location in a limited period of time, saying nothing, and makes a single change that moves the story forward.

Back? Let's move on to our third and final practice scene. Two characters this time. One change (it's always one change.) Here we go:

❖ ❖ ❖

He grinned at me from across the table. "I promised myself I'd never hire you."

"And why is that?" I didn't return his smile; I'd never much cared for him, and I liked him even less when he was sitting across the table from me in my little tavern, in my corner.

"I always figured you wouldn't be the type who'd mix business with pleasure — and I promised myself the day we were introduced that you and I were going to be the best of friends."

I sipped my drink and studied him through narrowed eyes. "You shouldn't make promises you can't keep — not even to yourself."

He laughed, not put off by my manner. But he was that sort — the kind of man who refused to believe that a woman might not find him attractive, might not be flattered by his attentions; might, in fact, prefer her own company to his. Insults rolled off his oblivious shoulders because he simply refused to believe a woman might mean them.

I meant them.

"You and I would have had a great time."

Only if he was lying on the floor and I was kicking him in the kidneys, I thought. "What do you want?"

"I want you to find my wife," he said. "She's been missing for two days, and I can't go to the police."

I leaned back, almost unable to breathe. He had a wife? Some poor woman had married this shmuck? I took a hard pull on my drink, feeling the soothing burn down the back of my throat. "Your wife. And why, exactly, can't you tell the police she's missing?"

He gave me a weak smile. A dead-fish-on-a-plate smile. He cleared his throat, and his gaze darted away from mine, and he said, "I hired mumble mumble mumble...."

I didn't catch it, and the part of it I did catch, I didn't quite believe. "One more time," I told him. "And this time, tell me so I can hear you."

He still didn't meet my eyes. In fact, he was staring at the ring on his left hand like it was the key to the kingdom of heaven. He said, "I hired these guys to kill her."

Yeah. That was what I thought he said. "And you want me to find the body?"

He shook his head. "She's still alive."

"I see," I said, not seeing at all.

"They took her," he told me, "but they didn't kill her. They're blackmailing me with her. They said they're going to tell her that I hired them to kill her, and they're going to turn her loose just outside of a police station, unless I pay them one million dollars."

"Ah." It became clearer.

"I want to get her back before they tell her. For that, I need you."

The change here is gradual. We know the main character doesn't like the man who wants to hire her, and we gradually get a feel for why — he seems slimy. We find out that he's married, and this confirms to us that he's definitely not the right man for our hero — her instincts are good. *Then,* however, we discover that he's the sort of guy who would hire people to kill his wife, and we suddenly realize that our character shouldn't even think about working for this scumball — except, if she doesn't, who's going to save his poor wife?

We go from disliking this guy a little to disliking him a lot. As changes go, it's fairly small, but enough to give us a complete scene and to move the story forward.

Your Turn

Two characters, one setting, a period of from five to ten minutes in which something happens that changes their relationship with each other and turns the story in a new direction. Here are some directions you can take:

hate ⊥ love
fear ⊥ trust
anticipation ⊥ dread
belief ⊥ disbelief
joy ⊥ sorrow
anger ⊥ amusement
trust ⊥ distrust

There are a million more of these. You might want to make a list of them — it can come in useful when you're stuck on a scene and you need a few prompts that can get you unstuck.

The big thing to remember in writing a scene — any scene — is that it isn't a scene until something changes; and once something changes, it's time to move on.

The Character Workshop: Designing A Life

I've designed this little workshop to help you sneak up on character development. Answer the questions in order, and take your time. Allow yourself as much space as you need to answer each one — some only require one-word answers, but some require a fair amount of page space to be answered completely. A word of warning — this isn't a complete character checklist; it's a workshop designed to break through stubborn preconceptions you might have had about characters you write and character design. Because of that, you will not have a complete character if you only answer the questions I've given you. And some of the questions are a little odd. Answer them anyway...at least the first time.

1. *Choose a gender.*

2. *Choose a place of birth.*

3. *Choose a hobby.*

4. *Choose a past job.*

5. *Choose a present job.*

6. *Choose a past love interest.*

7. *Choose an enemy.*

8. *Choose a pet.*

9. *Why is your character not working at the old job?*

10. *Why is your character not with the old love interest?*

11. *Why does your character not make the hobby a profession?*

12. *How did your character make the enemy?*

13. *How did the pet once save the character's life?*

14. *What is the one thing in the world your character would do anything to avoid? Why? What has he already done to avoid this? What do you see him doing in the future to avoid it?*

15. *What is the one thing in the world your character would do anything in the world to have? Why? What has he already done to try to obtain it?*

16. *What does he hope to try in the future?*

17. *What is your character's name? What is your character's age, and physical description.*

18. *Write everything else you know about your character, right now.*

And that's it. You should have several handwritten pages of information on your new character, and plenty of ideas about the story he could be in, and the role he could play in it. Good luck with this. I hope you've found it useful.

WORKSHEETS: No worksheet for this workshop. Use your writing notebook.

Deeper People: Putting Yourself Into Your Characters

A lot of fiction by beginning writers, and unfortunately a significant amount of fiction by published writers, is plagued by **paper people** — characters who never really come to life on the page. The published writers who still get away with this do so because they've learned to tell a story so compelling that editors will buy from them anyway. Beginners really don't have that luxury, and paper people will kill a sale as fast as anything.

Paper people fall into categories, and that is much of their problem.

You have Evil Villains, Oppressed Virginal Heroines, Naïve-But-Stalwart Heroes, and Smart-Ass Sidekicks, among other common types. (Depending on genre, you'll meet Hookers-With-Hearts-of-Gold, Strong-But-Silent Sheriffs, Nubile-Young-Secretaries-Who-Always-Think-They're-Too-Thin, Brilliant-But-Distracted Scientists, Ever-Dedicated Cops, and the inescapable Fearless Soldiers.) You recognize them as I list them, and can probably name as many novels where they feature prominently as I can.

They're recognizable as types, but they aren't recognizable as people. Real people have interests both broad and deep, friends and enemies from as far back as when they were two years old, hobbies that have absolutely nothing to do with their current Quest for the Silver Nematode, and the occasional pet, favorite book, and favorite song.

> *More than anything else, living characters have passions, hungers and desires, and they aren't all related to the story of the moment.*

Flat characters begin and end with whatever they're doing in the story.

Here's how to test your character to see if you have any hope of breathing some life into him as he stands. Write down the characteristics he has to have to successfully complete the story you've plotted out for him. You'll probably have things in there like "Intelligence," "Deep knowledge of spaceship construction and navigation," and "The ability to fire weapons accurately even while hanging upside-down by the ankles and with hands bound."

Hey, my characters can do some nifty things, too. Part of the fun of writing is writing people who are better at cool things than you are.

But if your character starts and ends with the things that will help him get through his mission, you have created *Yet Another Paper Person*.

YAPP. Bad. YAPPs don't sell books.

I'm going to show you the method I use to make my people real. It gets a bit personal; when I occasionally complain about writing being like dancing naked on your rooftop, this is the part of writing that most closely fits that description. This takes some courage. But it works.

You're going to put yourself into your characters. Not just the public things that you're proud of, like having won the fifth-grade statewide spelling bee, or being president of your graduating class and the person voted Most Likely To — but the things you wish you never had to admit to anyone, like the fact that you screwed up four marriages and three of the four were almost entirely your own fault.

Or that fact that you had a teenage pregnancy, and a teenage abortion. Or adoption.

The fact that you had an affair you never told anyone about.

The stupid stuff, too, like the fact that you couldn't carry a tune on a stretcher with two paramedics helping you. The fact that you whistle La Bamba in the shower. The fact that you absolutely, positively refuse to look at your butt in a mirror, clothed or unclothed, because you just hate it. The fact that you wear glasses, or are balding, or have dimples on your thighs and stretch marks from four pregnancies in which you frequently mistook yourself for the Hindenburg.

This workshop is private. In this voyage of discovery, you're going to have to be brutally honest, and you'll do that better with no one looking over your shoulder. Don't panic. Once you've been honest, I'll show you how to lie to disguise the truth and still have it be true to the story. First though, you have to be honest.

Here we go.

Part One of the Workshop

A. Write ten things about yourself that you think are fantastic things that you don't think other people really appreciate fully about you, or that they haven't noticed, or that they simply don't know about. Ten. Really.

B. Write ten things about yourself that would embarrass you terribly if anyone else knew about them. These can be things you have done, things you have wanted, things you have thought, fantasies you have entertained, or secrets you have been keeping. Doesn't matter. The only thing that matters is that you tell the truth. If it doesn't hurt and make you uncomfortable to write each of these, you aren't digging deep enough.

C. Describe your body as honestly as you can what you like about it, what you hate about it, and what you hope no one has noticed.

D. Describe five of the most wonderful moments of your life things you still look back on with pleasure and joy.

E. Describe five of the most painful moments of your life mistakes you've made, people you've hurt, things that you will probably regret until you die.

F. Write the ten things you are most passionate about. These can be religious, political, philosophical, personal, romantic — these are your causes. You can be in favor of them, or against them, but they have to matter to you. They don't have to be big; they just have to be yours.

Part Two of the Workshop

Okay. Enough soul-searching. You'll have to do this from time to time, but if you've done the exercise honestly this time, you now have enough goodies to give a whole novel or three full of characters with resonance and depth.

Obviously, you are not going to transfer any of this stuff directly into your novel. You're going to change it, transform it, invert it, spread it out around a whole bunch of people who are not like you. Yes, to do good work, you have to put yourself into your writing, but no, you don't have to put yourself in _recognizably_.

Let's say that one of the really tough-to-deal-with moments in your life came when you caught your girlfriend of five years cheating on you with her girlfriend. Ouch. You aren't going to get over that one any time soon. You've spent time wondering what was wrong with you, how many other people knew what was going on, if you were a laughingstock, if she'd ever done this before, with whom...and those questions aren't going to go away.

So give them to one character.

Give them to a character who is otherwise unlike you: different gender, or different sexual orientation, or different interests. Make the situation in which he or she finds out about the cheating via an entirely different method. If you're writing a novel about a female vampire-hunting space captain, and she's carrying around these feelings of yours, they aren't going to be your feelings anymore. They'll be hers.

Give her relationship with the cheater some backstory, make it as closely or distantly related to the plot as you wish, but get it in there. She has a life outside of chasing vampires through space, and sometimes her anger at what this person has done to her is going to find itself displaced onto innocent people who for one reason or another will remind her of the cheater. This will affect, to greater or lesser degree, her movement through the story. And it will — because it is personal and true, even if disguised — resonate with your readers.

For you to be able to use the events from your own life effectively in fiction, you must, then, do the following things:

1. Search out those events in your life that have meaning to you;

2. Honestly explore how each of those events affected you;

3. Disguise the events and your reactions to them while still maintaining their essential, emotional truth;

4. And give these altered events to your characters, both good and bad, as part of their personal histories.

And a final, essential point.

If this isn't hard for you to do, you aren't digging deeply enough.

The things that matter are never easy.

If you include what matters in your fiction, though, you'll sell better, reach your readers, and write something that isn't just the next *Paper Hero Goes on A Quest* doorstop novel. Say goodbye to Evil Villains, Oppressed Virginal Heroines, Naïve-But-Stalwart Heroes, and Smart-Ass Sidekicks forever.

Because once you put yourself into your characters, they become Deeper People.

They become real.

Notecarding: Plotting Under Pressure

Here's the scenario. You find yourself in a situation where you have to do a book in a hurry. Could be you got a letter back from an editor or agent telling you that, while they can't use the book you submitted, they would like to see your next project. Could be you took on more contracts than you have time to complete. Could be you forgot about a pending deadline, or put it off because Real Life intruded in a big way.

In any case, now you're faced with a book that must be done to a professional level in a severely limited amount of time, and, for real fun, let's say that you don't even have any idea yet what the book is going to be about. Maybe you know most of the characters, if it's a book in a continuing series. Maybe the whole thing is just a vague, nebulous blur in your mind — you sort of know what you'd like it to be about, but beyond that, you're in the dark.

Maybe you haven't a clue. You are as blank as the page in front of you. Maybe you simply have never been able to plot out a novel in advance and would like to try it.

No matter what your situation, don't panic. This workshop will teach you how to create plots out of thin air, with nothing but work, and more work, and maybe a bit of work after that. Sound fun? Well, actually, it is.

Preliminaries

In order to create this plot out of thin air, you're going to have to do a bit of book dissection. You're going to have to guess about following things in advance:

- Who are the primary viewpoint characters in the book?

- How long do you want the book to be?

- How long do you want each scene to be?

If you've never written a book before, I'll give you some help with this out. A viewpoint character is the one through whose eyes you see some or all of the action in a novel.

In books told in the first person — **The dragon was coming after me — flying close and tight behind me, with the flames of its breath heating up my heels as I ran** — you *usually* have only one viewpoint character, the narrator (though I have broken this rule in my novels *Talyn* and *Hawkspar*).

In books told in the third person — **The dragon shot around the corner after Erin, flapping hard and breathing fire at his heels** — you can have any number of viewpoint characters, but for the best flow of the book, you should spend most of your time with just a few. One to six viewpoint characters is pretty manageable. The hero, the sidekick, the villain, the love interest, the villain's sidekick, and even the hero's cat are all potential viewpoint characters.

Create more characters than you think you'll need, pick out the ones that really sing to you, and move on to the next step.

How long should the book be? Barring guidelines or contract clauses that state otherwise, figure on something between 90,000 and 125,000 words. You may end up going higher, but don't plan on going lower — novels shorter than 90,000 words are hard as hell to sell. *Unless you self-publish. Shorter self-published novels sell just fine.*

How long do you want each scene to be? Depends on your writing style and a lot of other things, but to get all the goodies that you need into a scene, you generally have to give yourself a bit of elbow room. Figure on more than a thousand words and less than five thousand. If you aren't sure how to create scenes, or what you need to have in one, do the **Scene Creation Workshop** a couple chapters back or read any number of excellent books or articles by me or other authors on the subject.

The Mathematics of Magic

I'm going to start a demo book for you, just so you can see how this goes.

I'm going to create four characters who will be my viewpoint characters. My heroine, named Elsie, is a twenty-something housepainter who recently lost her best friend. The hero is Mike, a sturdy, intelligent businessman bored out of his skull by the mundane nature of his existence. Mike's best friend is a free spirit with a tendency toward trouble named Frisco. And the villain is... hmmmm. Let's go weird with this, and make the book a paranormal. Let's say the villain is Elsie's dead best friend, who has been involved in wickedness that Elsie never knew about, and who ended up dead because of Elsie making an error — if things had gone the way this best friend planned, Elsie would have been dead, and the friend would have been... something else. Let it rest. The friend needs a name. Let's call her Annabelle.

Knowing nothing more about that, I'm ready to do a little math. Let's say that I want my book to be 100,000 words long, and I want each scene to run an average of two thousand words.

BOOK MATH FORMULA ONE:

Number of words Scene length in words = Number of Scenes

I'll need fifty scenes to complete the book. I have four characters through whose eyes we'll be discovering the story. I don't want to give each of them equal time, though — I want to spend most of the time with my hero and my heroine, only seeing the action through the eyes of the sidekick and the villain from time to time.

So say that I give my hero one third of the scenes, and my heroine one third of the scenes, and split the remaining third equally between sidekick and villain.

To do that, I'll divide my fifty scenes into thirds.

50 3 = 16 with a remainder of 2

For the moment, ignore the remainder and concentrate on sixteen. That's how many scenes Mike and Elsie will have. Annabelle and Frisco divide the final third between them. 16÷2 = 8, so they'll each get eight scenes. And you have that remainder of two — you can pass out the final two scenes to whomever you'd like to have them. I'm going to give an extra one to Annabelle, and one to Frisco.

So here's what we have:

CHARACTER	# OF SCENES
Elsie	16
Mike	16
Frisco	9
Annabelle	9

Break Out the Index Cards

This next bit is pure fun.

Get out a pack of index cards, write the name of each character on the correct number of cards, and if you'd like, on a few extras — I'll make eighteen for Elsie and Mike, ten or eleven for Frisco and Annabelle.

Once the names are on the cards, pull out a card set — I start with the secondary viewpoint characters, because this lets me let the main story float for a while, building up momentum.

With one set of character cards in hand, start writing down one-sentence scene ideas, one per card. Be a little crazy — just write down all the fun things that you can think of that could happen to the character you have in hand, keeping in mind that all scenes require conflict and change.

Here's a demo:

- **Frisco** — playing with the Ouija board alone, runs into the ghost of Annabelle, who tries to seduce him to her cause.

- **Frisco** — running with Mike, confesses that he's been using the Ouija board and has had some cool experiences; invites Mike to try the thing out.

- **Frisco** — meets Elsie and both likes her and has a bad feeling about her, as if he's seeing her through two pairs of eyes — he decides to see if he can get to know her better.

- **Frisco** — and Mike take Elsie snowboarding, and Frisco makes a careless mistake that almost gets Elsie killed; afterward, he cannot figure out how he made that error.

And so on. These are not written in any particular order, though you'll find that as you're throwing down ideas, some will fall into a clear linear order. Some won't. Don't worry about it. Never deny yourself a scene just because you can't figure out how it will fit.

Do cards for each of your characters. Don't worry about referring to the other cards as you put these scenes down — just let yourself have fun with them, coming up with one-line descriptions of exciting scenes that you want to write. As you get a few things on paper, you'll find that you start having ideas for other characters. And a rough idea for the story itself will start forming, too — what it's about, where it could start, how it could finish.

By the time you have all of your scene ideas on cards, you may have a clear idea of how the story will go. Or you may not. Doesn't matter. Find yourself a bit of floor spare, and put the cards on the floor, laying them out in the following fashion:

Elsie	Mike	Annabelle	Frisco
Elsie	Mike	Annabelle	Frisco
Cont.	Cont.	Cont.	Cont.

Don't worry when you're putting the cards out about placing them in any particular order — you'll get to that. Just keep them in character columns.

Now. There is probably one scene that stands out as the perfect scene to open the book — it might be from any of the characters' points of view, but when you think about what you want to read on the first page, one or two of the scenes will really stand out.

Put the scene that you prefer as your opener at the top of your row for that character.

Look through your other scenes for all the characters, and see which scenes, if any, are dependent on it, and which scenes for the other characters should be first for them.

Start putting things in order, leaving your scene cards in their character rows for the time being. You'll find that some of the scenes that you imagined being toward the end do remarkable things when moved to the beginning, and that your subconscious has given you some terrific correspondences — one character will be doing something that meshes beautifully but strangely with what another character is doing, giving the story depth that you did not anticipate.

You'll discover surprises — scenes that play off of each other to create humor or tragedy that you had not foreseen. You'll find a great deal of magic waiting as you shuffle your little squares of paper around.

You'll also find scenes that don't seem to fit, as well as some that strike you as dull or pointless. Scrap the dull or pointless ones, but don't give up on the ones that don't fit. By working in backstory, changing some of your plot around, and devising some deceptions and surprises, you can often create a place for the out-of-place scene that will add layers, depth, and power to your story.

Once you have your notecards in order by character, it's time to put them into one long, single line. Start with a strong scene, end with a strong scene, and in the middle make sure all your events could happen in the order in which you've placed them (though as you start typing this in, you can change things that don't quite work.)

Once the cards are in order and you've read through them once or twice to make sure you have them they way you want them, sit down at the computer, type them in using either outline or bullet format.

Copy and paste them into the bottom of your novel document. Now just look at each sentence-scene, write the scene that it describes, and delete it when you're done with it.

Working in this fashion, you eliminate all those get out of bed have a cup of coffee drive to work answer the e-mail and FINALLY something happens scenes that you can get otherwise. You're writing from exciting bit to exciting bit, trusting your brain and talent to tie everything in and to give you some great surprises along the way. You don't have an outline so much as you have a rather sparse roadmap, one that leaves plenty of room for adventure and that won't take the fun out of your story before you've even written it.

And you have something that can be completed on deadline, and that should be fresh and coherent and good when it's done.

Good luck with your project — and I hope you have as much fun with this technique as I have.

WORKSHEET NOTE: For folks who have access to index cards, buy several packs. I use Scrivener for most of what I do now, but this process I still do with real index cards.

If you live in a part of the world where index cards don't exist (as I've discovered many of my students do), print off as many copies of the worksheet for this lesson as you need (on the heaviest paper you can find) and cut along the dotted lines. Instant do-it-yourself index cards.

The Description Workshop

Description is a frequently-reviled writing skill.

It gets a bad reputation from books that include pages of turgid, extraneous detail; no book has ever been rendered unreadable by virtue of too little description. Unpublishable, maybe, but not unreadable. Whereas a couple of hundred-word descriptions jammed into a three-page paragraph can not only kill your book, but maybe even your editor or first reader. Bad.

So you don't want to do that. But you don't want to walk away from description entirely, either. It gives you powerful tools for bringing worlds and characters to life. Used judiciously, it can make your readers believe, and that is a wonderful thing.

You have a number of things you'll routinely have to describe in your writing settings, situations, and characters.

Let's do SETTING description first, since it's the first thing most writers think about when they think about description.

If you've done a lot of worldbuilding, it's easy to get carried away with this one. You've developed a ton of wonderful details, and the temptation is to use them all, and to do it all at once. At the beginning of your story, especially if you're doing a novel and are writing about your own world, you're going to have to give people some description so they'll know where they are. However, even in a solid block of description, if you keep the background moving, you'll bring the scene to life and keep your readers interest.

Here's an example of what I mean, taken from my novel *Diplomacy of Wolves*.

> *So Kait Galweigh stood off in one corner at the Dokteerak Naming Day party and scanned the crowed while she pretended to sip a drink. The Dokteerak Family women in their gauzy net finery clustered beneath the broad palms in the central garden, chatting about nothing of consequence. Torchlight cast an amber gleam on their sleek skins and pale hair and made the heavy gold at their throats and wrists seem to glow. They were decorative — Kait's Family had such women, too, and theirs was the fate she so desperately wished to escape. The senior diplomats from both Families, Galweigh and Dokteerak, gathered in the breezeway that surrounded the courtyard, leaning along the food-laden tables, nibbling from finger servings of yearling duck and broiled monkey and wild pig and papaya-stuffed python, telling each other amusing stories and watching, watching, their eyes never still. Concubines flirted and primped, tempting their way into berths in the beds of the high-ranking or the beautiful. Dokteerak guardsmen in gold and blue propped themselves against doorways, swapping racy stories and tales of bravado with Galweigh guardsmen in red and black. Outland princes and the parats of other Families and their cadet branches drifted from group to group, assessing available women the way hunting wolves assessed a herd of deer.*

(You can read the entire chapter here:

http://hollylisle.com/diplomacy-of-wolves

to see how I continued the use of people to describe setting.)

Now this is a longish paragraph — 214 words. However, the reader gets a feel for the world from watching people doing things.

Description Rule Number One: People are more interesting than scenery.

When you're finished reading this one paragraph, you have an idea of the social and political structure and technological level of this part of the world, social mores and morals, the weather that evening, the climate of the region, and at least a suggestion of the social standing of the characters. And if I've done my job correctly, you're interested enough in what the people are doing that you don't see the things I've slipped in with them. Did you consciously notice the palm trees, the presence of monkeys and papaya on the menu, the women dressed in gauzy clothing? Tropical climate. Did you notice concubines, decorative women, uniformed guardsmen, outland princes, Families with a capital F? Complex social structure with a number of conflicting political models, sexual mores different than those of middle-class America, and the presence of a definite hierarchy. Torchlight? The possibility, if not yet the certainty, of a lower-tech world. The Naming Day Party? An unfamiliar celebration of some sort and something that obviously is of some importance.

What other rules did I use in this paragraph?

Description Rule Two: Forms of the verb "to be" are your enemy.

I did not write, *It was a hot night*, or *The Dokteerak women were beautiful but immoral*, or *The food on the table was strange*. Those would have been really boring sentences.

If you're telling, you can't be showing, and when you describe something, you want to show it. You don't want to tell about it. Think about a car salesman. He wants you to buy the car. So does he tell you how great it is? No, he drags you out, sits your butt in the driver's seat, and lets you smell the leather interior, wrap your hands around the steering wheel, peer through the windshield, and feel the way it moves with you as you drive it through city streets.

Let your readers drive your world.

Exercise One:

List three or four important points about your story-universe that you want your readers to know. These can be anything from weather to political structure to the rules of a game characters will play that is integral to your plot. When you have them listed, write a paragraph describing them...but do it using people, and avoid as many variants of the verb *to be* as you can.

Finished? Like the energy in what you've done? Have you managed to sneak your worldbuilding in disguised as action? If you have, great. If not, give it another shot, and then let's move on.

Next, let's work on SITUATION description.

In order to start a story, you have to let the reader know where your character is, what the problem is, and why it matters. This requires description — but again, description shouldn't be something your reader has to drag himself through out of obligation. It should, instead, reach out of the page, grab him by the throat, and drag him kicking and screaming into your story and your world.

Here's a situation description I did for *Hunting the Corrigan's Blood*. It is, in fact, the first paragraph of the book, and this time it is straight description — no action.

> *The corpse's left eye squinted at me from mere centimeters away. Decomposition lent her face an increasingly inscrutable expression; the first time I'd regained consciousness, when I found myself tied to her, she looked like she had died in terror. After a while, she started leering at me, as if she had reached the place where I was going and took perverse pleasure from the thought that I would join her there soon. Now, having had her moment of amusement at my expense, she meditated; beneath thousands of dainty auburn braids, her face hung slack, bloated and discolored, the skin loosening. Threads of drool hung spiderwebbish from her gaping mouth. Her eyes, dry and sunken and filmed over beneath swollen lids, still stared directly at me.*

You can read this paragraph in context here:

http://hollylisle.com/hunting-the-corrigans-blood

to see how I used description to create situation.

Technically, it is a description of a dead body. However, it is a bit more compelling than a simple description of a corpse, because the narrator is telling you about the corpse in the first person while the she and the corpse are handcuffed together and locked in a locker.

It is, I think, one of the catchier openers I've done. From this short description, the reader understands immediately and completely that the narrator is in terrible trouble, that the trouble is premeditated and the stakes are high, and that there is at least a bit of a mystery ongoing — people don't refer to those they know as the corpse — so the dead body to which the narrator is bound must belong to a stranger. We get confirmation of that in subsequent paragraphs, but I've planted the seed in the first one.

So what rules did I follow in setting up this situation?

Description Rule Number Three: Lead with the biggest gun you've got.

I didn't start by mentioning that the narrator was badly hurt, though she was, and you get a hint of that from the fact that she's been unconscious more than once. I didn't lead with the locker, or with the narrator's confusion over the fact that the woman was a stranger, or with a description of the space station — or Cadence Drake's job, or any of the events that got her where she was. I started her out eyeball to eyeball with the body of a dead stranger, and took a bit of time and a number of gritty words to describe the stranger. (I also followed Rules One and Two.)

Exercise Two:

Figure out what the most compelling detail is in a situation you're trying to set up for your character. Weed out all the things you wish the reader knew, and all the things that are secondary, and just dig into that one compelling detail.

Finally, let's look at description of CHARACTER.

Everyone knows about this one —

> *Missy looked at herself in the mirror. She liked her short, pert nose, her perfectly blonde hair natural, of course and the way her enormous breasts complimented her tiny waist. She didn't think she was perfect, of course. She thought she was too skinny and plain, but everyone else kept insisting she was beautiful, so maybe she was.*

If you have ever written a paragraph like that, don't feel bad. Most of us have at one point or another. But it is dreadful, and there are much, much better ways to describe character.

I had to dig for an out-and-out description of a character, because I rarely do a block of text telling what a character looks like. I'll sneak a detail in here or there, but for the most part, I let characters describe themselves by their actions. Every once in a while, though, someone comes along who deserves a real description. This is from Chapter Two of **Diplomacy of Wolves**.

> *Crispin and Andrew both grinned at each other. As they did, Anwyn slouched into the dungeon. Marcue had thought from his name that he would be human. Anwyn was a good Parmatian name, like Crispin or Marcue, for that matter. The thing that skulked into the dungeon wasn't human, though. He might have been one of the Scarred — one of the creatures from the poisoned lands whose ancestors, stories said, had once been men. If he was Scarred, however, he was from no realm that had ever traded in Calimekka. And if he wasn't one of the Scarred, then he was a demon from the lowest pit of Zagtasht's darkest hell. Long horns curled out from his forehead. His scaled brow beetled over eyes so deeply set they looked more like hollow sockets. His lips parted in a grin that revealed teeth long as a man's thumb and serrated like a shark's. He hunched forward, and Marcue could make out the ridge of huge spines that ran down the center of his back beneath his cloak. His hands were talons, though five-fingered, and while one of his feet fit in a man's boot and grew from a man-shaped leg, the other was a cloven hoof attached to a leg that, beneath a man's breeches, bent backward at the knee. That leg he dragged forward as he moved into the room.*

231 words, most of it straight description. I used "to be" verbs in this, and interspersed a line-item description with reaction description from the scene's point-of-view character. The only reason I wrote the paragraph this way is because Anwyn isn't human, or anything like it, and I wanted to get that point across quickly and with as much visual and visceral impact as I could manage.

Description Rule Number Four: Describe by list only as a last resort.

Contrast the treatment above with the initial description of the young woman who is the actual focus of the scene.

> *The stone walls, rough-hewn and slime-coated, gleamed in the torchlight. The chill of the place, and the stink and the darkness and the skittering sounds of the rats, wore on Marcue's nerves even when all the cells were full and the men in them talked and quarreled and wondered about their futures. Now the dungeon was empty except for one prisoner, and that was a girl — a child, really — and she rarely spoke, but frequently cried. Her crying was worse than the rats.*

That's it. That's all you learn about her in the first paragraph. I dole out bits and pieces of descriptive information throughout the rest of the scene, so that by the end of it, the reader has a very clear picture of Danya Galweigh — but it comes only a line here and a line there. You can read all of Chapter Two here:

http://hollylisle.com/diplomacy-of-wolves-chapter-2

Take a look to see how description of a major character can be made subtle and spread out, and compare to how it can be blunt and in-your-face, and decide which way you want to present each character — and *why* — before you write your description.

Description Rule Number Five: Only describe what is different.

Don't waste your time cataloguing all the things in your world that are the same as all the things that match them in the world we know.

If it's the same, it's insignificant, and your reader will catch on quickly and start skimming your book, trying to find what matters.

The only things that matter are the things that are different.

While J.R.R. Tolkien is not the writer I would generally refer to as a paragon of concise descriptive prowess, he did not waste his time informing his readers that water was wet, that grass was green, or that trees were made of wood and had leaves. The trees he described in detail were the ones that walked and talked; he showed us the water in the swamp when it had the corpses of long-dead warriors staring out of it; and, the verdant green of the Shire was what he spoke of on the hobbits homecoming, as *what was different* after their trek through the hell of a demon's mad war.

Exercise Three:

List the characteristics that make your character different. When you have that list, write two samples — one in which you do straight description, and one in which you spread out the salient points about your character over paragraphs or pages.

Description doesn't have to be the part of your writing that readers skim to get to the good stuff. If you pay attention to the five basic rules of description, you'll make description part of the good stuff.

Pacing Dialogue and Action Scenes: Your Story at Your Speed

What is pacing?

Pacing is moving your story forward smoothly, at your speed. Not everyone wants a breakneck race through the pages; not everyone wants a bucolic amble, either. The goal of this workshop is to help you take control of your writing pace — to make your story travel at the pace you want, so that you can tell the story you want to tell.

Here are some techniques I've learned for controlling the pace of my stories.

To Speed Up Action Scenes:

Limit extraneous information.

This is not the time to describe the countryside, the weather, or what people are wearing. Concentrate on the main characters, their movements, their five senses, and their emotions as they work through whatever problem they're facing.

Pull your camera in close.

Let us taste the blood at the corner of the lip, feel the pain of the broken bone, hear the whistling of the blade, smell sweat, see eyes wide with shock, the beads of sweat on upper lips. Sense details create a sense of immediacy and urgency, and make a scene feel faster.

Keep sentences short and clean.

There are times and places for the hundred word sentence, but the fast-paced action scene is not one of them.

Be sharp, short, hard-edged.

Use fragments (sparingly). Kill adjectives and adverbs — be ruthless. You don't need many, and may not need any. Find good verbs and nouns, and let the scene run with them.

Examples of action scenes that play well quickly:

- Fight scenes
- Chase scenes
- Critical moments in your plot

To Slow Down Action Scenes:

Offer setting details.

Now you can take a bit of time with descriptive passages, narrative notes on culture, history or character background, local color, costuming, terrain details, and even the weather. Caution: To slow a scene to the point of inducing coma, add a lot of these.

Move the camera out.

Give us the panoramic view of the characters, their surroundings and their actions from either distant third person or omniscient viewpoint. We don't need to be inside their heads all the time, and being outside of their heads slows down the perceived pace of the scene a bit.

Give yourself a bit more room on sentence length.

If you want to experiment with the hundred-word sentence, you can do it here. Don't go overboard; your objective is still to tell a story and move the action forward. But you do have significant leeway in the slower scene. Moderate (stress MODERATE) use of adverbs and adjectives. Instead of none, you can scatter a few throughout the scene. This stuff in like fennel, though — a tiny pinch of *adjective* or *adverb* goes a long, long way.

Scenes that do well with a slower pace:

- Middle scenes
- Romantic scenes
- Developmental moments in the plot

Action Practice: Your Turn

Remember that any scene can be written with either a fast or slow pace — and either can work, depending on how it fits with the rest of your manuscript.

To get comfortable with looking at pace as something you control (instead of as something that controls you), you're going to write the same action scene two ways — first paced as quickly as you can, and then as slowly. If you have a scene in mind that you would like to try this with, use that. If you don't have any ideas, then you can write about either a fight between two people, or one character trying to get away from another character.

To accelerate a dialogue scene:

Get to the point.

Start in the middle of the conversation, with the first thing that a character says being directly related to the problem of the scene. Don't worry about describing how the characters meet up, or how they greet each other, or giving us their conversation before they get to the point. Be direct.

The conversation starts not with:

> "Hi, Bill."

> "Oh, hey, Fred. Good to see you today. Gorgeous weather, isn't it?"

But with:

> "I couldn't believe it when I heard that Keith Cavernaugh got murdered last night."

> Fred almost dropped his rake. "I hadn't heard," he said.

Avoid most description.

Don't spend a great deal of time telling us what the characters are doing while they're talking. A bit of this is necessary; otherwise you end up with two heads speaking into a void. But limit brutally. If someone is talking while hand-tooling a saddle, we don't need to know at that time the details of the leather design.

Allow characters to talk at cross-purposes.

Good listeners are nice in real life, but people who interrupt each other and don't listen because each is talking about what they think is most important get a lot of information on the page in a short space, and draw the reader in.

Example:

> "So then they found the murder weapon under the kitchen sink, but no one is talking about whether there were prints on it or not — "

"...Uh-huh. Anyway, Fred stood me up for our date, and then he had the nerve to show up three hours late with these droopy, sorry excuses for flowers and some lame excuse about his car breaking down."

Lisa sighed. "...So the police took his wife in for questioning this morning, and you have to think about her and those three sweet little children there in the house with him when it happened —"

"Who cares, Lisa? I'm telling you that Fred's a jerk, and you're telling about people I don't even know."

"We both already knew Fred was a jerk. The guy who was murdered lives right around the corner from you."

End the dialogue the instant you've achieved your objective.

If you wanted the conversation to throw doubt on the motives of one of the two speakers, bail out of it the instant the first speaker becomes suspicious of the second. Don't waste time getting them out of the conversation. Just cut to the next scene.

To slow down dialogue scenes:

Have characters meander and wander from point to point.

This especially works well in comic dialogue, and is something Mark Twain did especially well. Imagine conversations you have had with people who stopped and started, forgot what they wanted to say, remembered extraneous details that to them suddenly seemed like something they just had to let you in on.

Warning: A little of this goes a long way. Keep these meanderings pruned down unless you **want** your readers to want to murder the speaker.

Here's a link to *The Celebrated Jumping Frog of Calaveras County*:

http://etext.virginia.edu/railton/huckfinn/
jumpfrog.html

...which is an excellent example of what I'm talking about.

Use more description of what characters are doing, where they are, and so on.

Instead of:

> *"I'm not ready to get involved in a murder."*
>
> *"Then get ready, because you're already involved."*

Write:

> *"I'm not ready to get involved in a murder." Louise wouldn't meet her sister's eye. Instead she stood there in the kitchen with her back pressed up against the sink, and with the sun pouring in through the window catching the fly-away hairs that had escaped her ponytail, and polished the silver teapot that their mother had left her. The backlighting from the window made her look like some sort of middle-aged angel.*
>
> *Carolyn refused to be evaded. "Then get ready," she said, "because you're already involved."*

Let your characters be good listeners.

But not for too long. Having one person conveying information while the other person sits there supportively, adding little murmurs of understanding and appreciation, may be great in real life. But it's amazing boring to read about.

Go past your main point in concluding the dialogue.

Let the characters wander into other topics to hide the important information that you've conveyed — this works well for planting red herrings in mysteries and in making important story points subtle instead of emphasized. It's a great way to play fair and still sneak up on your reader with a surprise or two.

Dialogue Practice: Your Turn

Do two versions of a dialogue between two people, one of whom is holding information of life-or-death import. In the first version, get the information across quickly and with emphasis — make it exciting.

In the second version, hide the information in the middle of the dialogue, and make either the speaker not aware that he's let this info slip, or the listener not catch on to the import of what he's heard.

To write professionally, you must learn to make your dialogue feel real to your reader, while making sure it's carrying the information you need to present in ways you're reader won't recognize as presentation.

This takes practice. To get the hang of it, write dialogue as your warm up every day — ten minutes doing one type of dialogue, between any characters, for any story, or just about two strangers. Set your timer, write steadily.

You'll get there.

Holly Lisle

Maps Workshop: Developing the Fictional World Through Mapping

Most of the books I've written have started with a map.

Not with an idea, or a character, or a theme. With a hand-drawn map, doodled out first while I was sitting and keeping someone else company, or while I was on break, or when I couldn't think of what to write and had no ideas to speak of and knew that if I drew a map something would come to me. Some of the maps were fairly artistic from the start. Some began on napkins or the backs of throw-away paper, and only became things of any artistic merit after they'd served their initial purpose of handing me an idea for a novel.

If you want specific titles of books that began as maps, I give you *Fire in the Mist*, *Bones of the Past* and *Mind of the Magic* (the Arhel novels), *Sympathy for the Devil*, *The Devil and Dan Cooley*, and *Hell on High* (the DEVIL'S POINT novels), *The Rose Sea*, *Glenraven* and *Glenraven: In the Shadow of the Rift*, *Hunting the Corrigan's Blood*, *Curse of the Black Heron*, and finally the trilogy I'm currently writing, *Diplomacy of Wolves*, *Vengeance of Dragons*, and *Courage of Falcons* (the SECRET TEXTS trilogy.) In other words, you'd have to look through your stacks a bit to find a book I've written that didn't begin as a map.

Now I know this is a weird little quirk of mine, and I can't guarantee you that if you'll just draw a map, it will give you a novel that will sell. But on the chance that what works for me will work for you, too, I'll go through the steps I use in doing my maps, and maybe my process will spark something for you.

I have favorite tools for mapping. I like graph paper, and I like the drafting markers that you can get from Office Max or Office Depot for about six bucks a set that come in five thicknesses, from. 1 mm up to. 5 mm. (Tech-Liner Drawing Pen Set, from Alvin) I don't use pencil, ever, and while you're doing this workshop, you shouldn't either. If you like the technique but find the inability to erase a detriment instead of a plus, feel free to modify it, but at least this first time, do not give yourself waffling room. Use pen and grit your teeth.

This first map is going to be your continent. I frequently also draw city and town maps, and in some instances street maps. I usually draw floor-plans for ships, houses, and other indoor places where my characters will spend a lot of time. I've never written a book that didn't have mapping as one stage of its production. It's just that occasionally mapping is the second stage, or even the third — say around about the time I get the first two chapters written and realize there are important things about my characters' world that I do not know.

Before we get started, I want to be *very* clear about one issue that I know some of you are already sweating over. This doesn't have to be pretty. You do not get extra points for artistry. I'm showing you a technique for generating ideas and creating a story where you didn't have anything before, not trying to turn you into an illustrator. If you can't draw a straight line, no problem. You aren't going to need any straight lines. Wobbles are part of the process. Nobody but you ever has to see this map. Nobody but you ever has to know it even exists. It doesn't have to go in front of the book you're going to write, and if you decide you do want it in the front of your book, your publisher is going to hire an artist to redraw it, no matter how cool you made it look. So stop already with the complaining about how you can't draw.

Your Turn

Read all the following instructions before you start drawing, down to the line of dingbats (❖ ❖ ❖).

Then go back and draw your map.

- Get out your graph paper. Draw a dot. Draw another dot. Draw a third dot.

- Draw some upside-down V's in a line (but not necessarily a straight line). These are your mountain range. Name the range. You can have more than one. You can make it thick or thin. If you leave any gaps between the V's, these can become passes.

- Draw some snaky lines from the mountain range outward in a couple of directions. Name each snaky line "Something" River. (Do not be a smart-aleck and take this literally).

- Draw some broken (- - - -) lines separating at least two of the dots from each other. Call these borders. Name the states, counties, or countries on either side of each border.

- Add a couple of other things that you find appealing — maybe a lake or an ocean or a desert. If you give yourself a shoreline (another long, wavy, wobbly line) stick some islands offshore. Maybe doodle in a forest. I use those kindergarten cloud shapes to indicate forests. You know, a whole bunch of little puffy, fluffy thingees all crammed in together. To me, these look like a deciduous forest as seen from the air in the summer. At least, they come close enough to satisfy me.

- Now name the dots you've already drawn — they're major cities. Draw a few more dots in interesting places, and name them, too. They're towns. Draw two small squares in out-of-the-way places. These are ruins from previous civilizations. Call them whatever you want.

It's time to make use of your mistakes.

Find the places where you wanted to erase. You drew a line someplace where it didn't belong, (you right-angled off a river, maybe). That's okay. That right-angled thing was designed by engineers. Really it was. It's an aqueduct, or a canal, or a wall. You have a road that goes nowhere? That's cool — somebody made it, and it used to go somewhere, and now all you have to do is figure out who made it, and where it used to go, and why it doesn't go there anymore. You have a ruin-box in what accidentally became a lake, or an ocean? No problem. Once upon a time that ruin was above ground. Or maybe it wasn't, and once upon a time there was a civilization that lived under the water.

See what I mean about mistakes? They're a treasure-trove of story ideas waiting to happen.

Now...

Put the art supplies away and get out a few sheets of notebook paper, or sit down at your computer (I usually do this stage on paper, but that isn't essential). This is the essay portion of the workshop. Don't groan — this is a lot more fun than drawing the map was.

Answer the following questions, taking as much space as you need for each answer.

Why are the borders there? By this I mean, why do these people have borders in the first place? A border always implies that conditions, people, philosophies, governments, or something else is different on each side.

What goes up and down the rivers? (People, contraband, products?) How does it get there? Who takes it?

How are the people on one side of the border different from the people on the other side? (Religion, government, race, species... go into detail. Really take some time working out what these differences are, and put some effort into figuring out why they were important enough to necessitate the creation of that border.)

What lives in the mountains? (Animals, people, big scary things, all of the above?)

How does the weather endanger the lives of the people who live in your world? (Along with weather — stuff like tornadoes, droughts, hurricanes, snowstorms, avalanches, and so on, you should include things like areas where you'll have earthquakes and volcanoes. Don't be afraid to be generous in heaping out troubles. You'll find plenty of use for them.)

What else endangers the people on your continent? (Plagues, barbarians, people from the other side of the world, monsters from the

105

oceans or beneath the earth... Again, take some time on this. And be generous.)

Do a quick timeline in hundred year increments, for maybe two thousand years. Write down one really big thing that happened in each of those hundred-year periods. It can be geological, political, religious, magical, whatever. But it needs to be big. (Example: Invasion of the Sheromene headhunters into the country of Dormica, and subsequent decimation of the native population and establishment of the Sheromenes in the southern half of that country.)

Write whatever else you can think of right now. See where you're starting to get the feel for a novel? A big novel? Good. Keep moving back and forth, from your map to your notes. Add stuff to the map as it occurs to you. Add stuff to the notes until something inside your brain goes "ding" and lets you know that you have a book idea that you're genuinely excited about.

You can follow this same process with a single city. (You should have seen the map I did of Ariss — it was so cool. I started out with a compass, and drew something like ten concentric circles, called them walls, and filled in the spaces between with roads and buildings. And divided the city right in half. The first book I ever sold was born from those circles with the line right down the middle. I still get goosebumps thinking about it.)

Good luck. If this works for you and you get something you really like, let me know. I'd love to hear about it.

The Magic of Goals: How to Get There from Here

When I was twenty-five years old and sending out my first manuscript, I included in my query letter to agents the following little tidbit about my plans for my future — "I intend to write one romance novel a month."

You can laugh. Believe me, I do when I think back on my hubris. Granted, the **Holly Lisle Novel of the Month Club** was going to consist entirely of 60,000-word category romance novels. And granted, I was demonstrating the understanding that one novel was not going to constitute my life's work. But as agent after agent pointed out, if I intended to do twelve novels a year, the odds were that none of them were going to be very good.

But I did have goals. And once I learned more about writing, and about writing professionally, I was able to update them to create better goals. I would not have made it as a writer without goals — written out, put up where I could see them on the day I decided I was going to be a writer for real, and checked off as I reached them or updated as I changed them.

Goals change a vague dream into a plan of action. Clearly stated goals are the step between what you want and what you get.

When you complete this workshop, you'll have planned out your career and given yourself the steps to start it. Please understand that goals change over time, and the career you visualize today may not be anything like the career you want in a year, or five years. But we're going to plan for that, too.

We're going to define what good goals are, and evaluate which ones to keep and which ones to change and which ones to boot out the door. And then you're going to write your goals.

So. Let's get started.

Definition of Good Goals

Good goals have the following ten characteristics:

1. Good goals are describable.

There is nothing nebulous or vague about a good goal. A good goal is not a fairy-tale castle shimmering, half-described, at the edge of wakefulness. Good goals are not warm feelings, hot hunches, or a nagging itch down your spine. These are all fine and wonderful things, and they can inspire goals, but they are NOT goals. A good goal is concrete, plain, stark, explainable in words of one syllable to people who know nothing about what you hope to do. Good goals require neither the word 'thing,' nor wild hand gestures to get across. "I'm going to write a 100,000-word fantasy novel" is an acceptable starting goal. As for "I'm going to, ah, do this thing, ah, where, a, I sit down and listen to my MUSE, and ah, await inspiration…and then I'm going to internalize… ::gesture, gesture:: …," No. Saints preserve us, no.

You cannot hit a target you cannot clearly see. Words of one syllable. Two syllables tops. Trust me.

2. Good goals are positive.

You can look at this as Norman Vincent Peal-ism or tap-dancing into the realm of the metaphysical or just as addressing your subconscious, but when you set goals, only set positive goals — things you want to do, not things you want to avoid.

"Don't write trash" is a bad goal. The subconscious mind hears only positives — it'll hear "Write trash" as your goal. What it will do with the goal it hears is hard to say, but it won't get you where you want to go. "Write my best work every time" is the same goal phrased in a way that will help you reach it.

3. Good goals excite you.

You'll find yourself thinking about a good goal at times far removed from the actual process of achieving them. If sailing around the world is a good goal for you, you'll find yourself cheerfully contemplating all the steps that you'll need to take to achieve that goal. If writing a novel is a good goal for you, you'll find yourself considering characters and plot and conflict and imagining how they'll go together while flipping burgers at your day job or arguing with your employee or necking with the love of your life. (Worse, you'll figure out how to work necking with your beloved into the book.)

Good goals arise from your dreams, from the picture you hold of yourself in your heart and mind. Good goals are born from the part of you that yearns to be heroic; they are the path you take from the person you are to the person you want to become.

4. Good goals belong exclusively to you.

This is related to #1, but not the same. Your goals have to be your own. So if your mother always dreamed of having a doctor in the family, and your father can see you as an architect, while you faint at the sight of blood and couldn't care less whether a house is made of adobe or brick so long as it keeps the rain out, it's time to take action.

Help your mom find some financial aid so she can apply to medical school, buy your dad a drafting table for Christmas, but realize that this life is the only one you can be sure you get, and you cannot spend it fulfilling other people's dreams. Not even the people who love you most, wonderful though your folks, your spouse, or even your kids undoubtedly are.

Yes, they want the best for you. But they can't know what that is, simply because they're not you. Is this selfish? Maybe. But it's also self-preservation. Ask people with careers they never wanted — that they let their parents or spouses or guidance counselors pick out for them — to tell you about their lives. I've spent years doing this. You'll hear about ninety-five tales of misery for every five that worked out okay.

Don't go there. *Your* passions, *your* life, *your* goals, dammit — because if you don't follow them, no one will.

5. You can achieve good goals by your own actions.

Deciding to win a Hugo or a Pulitzer or to hit the New York Times bestseller list are bad goals. Nice dreams, especially nice if they become reality. But bad goals. Why? Because nothing you can do can make them happen. You can write brilliant novels, editors can love them, publishers can bring them out in wonderful editions, bookstores can stock them by the zillions, and readers can buy them in vast numbers and adore you as the Second Coming of Twain — but whether or not the New York Times deigns to notice you or award committees give you a second look is something you cannot hope to control.

Goals dependent entirely on the actions of others are destructive. If you set out to win an award and you don't, you'll take the hit for a failure — but it isn't the sort of failure that has any up-side. When an editor rejects your novel, you can do something about that. You can revise, resubmit, figure out where you went wrong and learn from it. When an award committee passes you over, it says nothing about your work and everything about the award committee. But you still see yourself as having failed. And you don't need that.

6. You can lay out the path to a good goal.

Writing a novel may or may not be a good goal for you. If you can look at it and say, "Okay, first I'll do worldbuilding and then a timeline, then develop some characters and put together a plot based on who my characters are and what they need, then I'll outline my story and then I'll write a thousand words a day on the first draft…" then writing a novel is a good goal for you. If you just say, "My goal is to write a book," but you see writing a book as a single task, then writing a book is likely to be a killer reef of a goal — one that sinks you.

7. You reach good goals regularly.

You're on the right track if, when you break down your big goal into smaller goals, you actually accomplish the smaller goals. If you're setting 3000 words a day as one of your goals, and you're writing 500 words a day, rethink. There's nothing like the forced failure of impossible goals to make you want to roll over and die. Or at least flush your dreams down the toilet and walk away forever.

You're going to hit good goals, the same way your feet hit the treads running up stairs. Nobody makes the rise on stairs three feet tall, because nobody could use stairs like those. Make the steps you build for your career usable. If your goal is a certain number of words and it's the right goal for you, then every day, or almost every day, you'll sit down and reach your goal, and feel great when you're done. Maybe you'll run a bit over — but you'll know that you did enough, and you'll be ready to do the same thing tomorrow. It's like doing the right amount of exercise; when you're finished, you should feel like it would be fun to do the same thing all over again.

8. Good goals leave you hungry.

Hunger is what got you into this in the first place, of course. Hunger to do more than you're already doing, to be more than you were yesterday, to create something wonderful. Good goal are going to address that hunger. Write goals for yourself that send a little chill down your spine. Pretend you're a little kid, and the world is brand new and everything is possible. Then look at all the endless possibilities, and identify the ones that give you goosebumps. Pick those. Tell yourself 'I want to do that.'

9. Good goals withstand repeated kicking.

Bad news. The world is ungentle with dreamers. It injects repeated reality into the dreamspace you build for yourself, and until you reshape the world to fit your vision, you can expect a certain amount of...er... hostility. Scorn. Derision. Even after you've succeeded, the world will come after you. People, much as they like success stories, also like disaster movies, and more than a few will be happy to leap in and trash you. Your goals are going to have to bear up under assault from both expected and unexpected fronts.

Beyond active opposition, you're also going to hit low points, bad markets, changes in tastes, and other things that can really hurt you. Failure is a necessary part of success — it tells you you're still daring to take chances. But failure and rejection hurt. Good goals will help you fall back and regroup, focus past the obstacles and give you something to shoot for even when times are hard.

Now the good news. If you've chosen the right goals, your response to repeated attacks, obstacles, and crashes will be something along the lines of 'Don't think I can do it? Just watch me.' (Sometimes you get to roll up in a corner and whimper like a whipped puppy for an hour or two first — but no more. Chin up. Remember, these are your goals. They're worth hanging onto.)

Remember, **every successful career belongs to the person who survived it.**

10. Good goals make you happy.

Most days you should be rolling out of bed ready to go, excited about what you're going to be working on. If your first thought about your work or your goals is, "Oh, God, again?" you're doing the wrong thing, or doing the right thing the wrong way.

The Goal-Writing Exercise

Let's get to work putting your goals together.

A note — and I cannot over-stress the importance of this. You must write your goals down, in permanent form, in a place where you can find them and see them and acknowledge them. Goals that you just hold in your head are as worthless as goals you can't find the words to describe — you think you know where you're going, but when you actually try to figure out where you are, everything goes up in smoke.

So. Get a pen. Get some good paper, or a notebook, or a stack of index cards. (Or download your worksheets and print of a handful of the page for this lesson).

These goals are your promises to yourself that your dreams are more than just dreams, and like any good lawyer, you're going to get your promises in writing.

Step 1

Now. We're going to play a game for a minute. Close your eyes and see yourself working — ten years from now — with a smile on your face. You're pushing yourself hard because you're doing the thing you love. You've been at it for long, long hours because the work has to be done now, but also because working hard at the right thing is a joy. No one has to smack you with a time-card or a stack of bills to get you out of bed in the morning. You'd be doing this for free, except that ten years into the game, you're making decent money.

What are you doing? When you have a clear picture, open your eyes and write it down.

Are you playing pro hockey? Seeing your fifteenth five-year-old with chicken pox that day? Hammering shingles on a roof? Writing your twentieth novel?

It doesn't matter what you're doing, so long as you're working. Until you can see yourself working at something and loving the work, don't go on to Step 2.

Step 2

You've seen yourself in ten years, and you have a waypoint that looks good to you. Now you have to figure out how to get there.

I'm going to take writing as your long-term goal because this workshop is about writing; if you've discovered that writing isn't your future, hang in with me here, anyway, though, because this workshop will at least give you your first roadmap toward the future you want.

So. Say you're going to be writing novels professionally in ten years. How do you get there?

1) Break down your vision of the future into its component parts

Say your first goal is Complete my first novel by the time I'm twenty-five. (This was my first big goal, so I'm including it as my example. I wrote it down in my journal on a whim, in list of New Year's resolutions in 1985, when I was twenty-four. I gave myself ten months to learn how to write a novel, and to actually get the thing done.)

Break down that big goal — because in its current form, it's meaningless. Write a novel? I know people who have been "writing a novel" for the last thirty or forty years. They haven't actually put their words on paper yet, mind you — but they're certain that what they're doing is going to make them the biggest thing since J.K. Rowling, just as soon as they do the trivial little task of scribbling out their work of immortal literary genius. "I have it all in my head," they say. You might know some of them, too. Don't be them. They'll dream forever, and never wake to do.

Instead, dissect your dream into workable pieces. The component parts of writing a novel are writing, researching, worldbuilding, developing characters, plotting, revising, finding markets, and submitting the completed work. Each of these segments can become a perfectly good goal, if written correctly.

Take "writing". Because if you hope for a writing career you must write regularly, write your goal so that it includes both how often and how much you must write to reach your larger goal.

My first writing-process goal was *Write every day*. It didn't work very well for me. I only had half of what I needed to make it a good goal. I wrote every day, but without including a "how much?" limit, I never knew when I had done enough. So no matter how much I wrote, I was always unsatisfied with myself.

When I changed the goal to *Write ten pages every day*, I discovered that I was on to something. Some days I wrote more, but I knew that extra was gravy, there just because I was having fun. Some days I didn't make my ten pages. And there were days when I couldn't write at all because of emergencies and the intrusion of Real Life. But I came close to ten pages a day every day, and that was good enough.

I finished my first novel before my twenty-fifth birthday, in spite of writing it on a manual typewriter, and doing over nine hundred pages of typing for what turned out to be a 60,000-word book (about 240 manuscript pages in the format I was then using).

I learned a lot from the process, and even though that first book never sold, it was worth doing. I learned a lot about writing, about marketing myself, and about failure. I also discovered that I had found the thing I wanted to do for the rest of my life.

2) Put the parts into a logical order

After you've figured out what the steps to achieving a big goal are, you need to put them in order. One logical order for the necessary steps in my writing a novel example would be:

- Research the necessary background in two weeks.

- Build the world in preliminary form in three weeks, creating one world map, one city map, three major culture descriptions with religion, language, and history notes (3 single-spaced pages per culture), and a flora and fauna list of twenty-five interrelated species, with descriptions.

- Develop my main characters — four protagonists (the good guys) and four antagonists (the bad guys), in four days, doing one single-spaced first person biography for each one.

- Plot out the story in one week, using line-per-scene format, planning each scene at two-thousand words and the whole book at 100,000 words.

- Write the first draft of the book at 2000 words per day, finishing the first draft in fifty working days.

- Revise the first draft in one month, using one-pass revision techniques.

- Find publishers that accept unagented queries for this type of novel, and send two query letters a day until I have covered my field of first choice publishers.

- Print and submit a copy of the novel to interested editors; write a cover letter and have the manuscript in the mail no more than three days following an editor's go-ahead.

- Query recommended AAR-member agents to find an agent who will agree to negotiate my first contract, if the book sells; see if the agent would consider representing my other work in the case that the first novel does sell.

Another acceptable way of doing this would be:

- Write five pages of my 100,000 word novel a day, doing necessary worldbuilding, character and plot development as I write. Finish first draft in 100 working days.

- Revise the first draft in one month, using one-pass revision techniques.

- Find publishers that accept...

And so on.

3) Give yourself a time frame

For your big goals, a general time frame is fine.

> *One year — Will have written first novel.*

> *Five years — Will have written and submitted ten novels...*

For your smaller goals, be more specific. Sit down and figure out how you work, and more importantly, how you want to work based on what you're capable of. Always include completion times for each goal.

4) Include both big goals and the steps to reach them in your plan

You can do goals for writing the books, for selling them, for the amount of money you want to make, for quitting your day job and writing full time. Remember, you cannot hit a target you cannot clearly see (at least not repeatedly) — so if you want to work up to making six figures annually, make that a goal, and then figure out what steps you're going to have to do to get there.

5) Provide a way of tracking your progress

I'm going to make a recommendation here that worked like magic for me. You don't have to follow it; I can't guarantee that it will be so spectacular for you. But I'm putting it out there anyway, because it might.

Get index cards, push pins, and a largish cork board. Write each of the big goals you've set for yourself and each of your step goals separate index cards, using the following format:

Goal	Complete my first novel by my twenty- fifth birthday
Date goal set	Jan. 1, 1985
Target date	Oct. 8, 1985
Date achieved	Oct. 1, 1985

Pin each of your goals on the cork board in a logical order — first novel at the top left, million-dollar-a-year income at the bottom right, for example — and put the cork board up where you can see it from where you work. Keep good track of your progress. Reward yourself for achievements like first submission, first acceptance, first advance check, first publication day. Some of these you may want to put on a calendar and celebrate every year.

6) Be kind to yourself

Remember that you have to build your steps so that they're usable, you have to accept that every success is born of repeated failures, and that if this were easy, everyone would do it.

You have to set goals that you want. *Really* want. That you are willing to undergo deprivation, hardship, and disappointment to achieve.

Don't beat yourself up when you fail. Remind yourself that you have the guts to pursue your dreams — sadly, most people don't — and that simply the fact that you're tough enough to fight for what you want makes you and your life and your goals worth celebrating.

There is no failure in fighting and losing if you get up and fight again. There is only failure in quitting — in walking away and leaving your dreams to die.

Fight, and plan to win. You can do it. You're tougher than you think.

Follow the steps above, and write out your first goals now.

SECTION III
Writing & Selling

How to Start Writing, and Keep Writing, and Write What Matters to You

In **Writing & Selling**, you'll discover a number of thinking obstacles writers create for themselves that hurt their writing and their careers — and explore which of these may plague you and how you can fix them.

You'll also dig into processes that will allow you to create fiction you love and want to write enough that it will make getting out of bed in the morning (or evening — whatever your schedule) an adventure you look forward to just about daily.

Your Book Is Not Your Baby

I've heard a lot of writers refer to their books as their babies. And many have even extended the analogy further — they say they gestate the thing for nine months, go through terrible pain to get it out into the world...and then it never calls or writes, and when it's out on its own, it doesn't become a rich doctor as they had hoped it would, but instead bums around the beach and drinks cheap wine out of a paper bag.

It's a cute analogy. But it doesn't have much to do with writing a book. I've written books, and I've had babies, and as I, (and a whole bunch of chagrined sixteen-year-old girls) could tell you, once the baby is planted, you don't really have to do a whole lot to make sure it arrives nine months later. It will come whether you're ready or not.

Unlike babies, books will not arrive if you sit around on you butt watching soap operas or reading the funnies or talking on the phone to your girlfriends. Books arrive only if you expend concentrated effort over a long term. Every day you have to hold what you wrote the day before and the week before and the month before in the back of your mind, and simultaneously you have to keep a part of your focus on what you intend to write the next day, and the next week, and the next month.

If short-story writers are like sprinters, and the writers of novellas are like milers, then novelists are marathoners. The ones who write books over 150,000 words are the Iron Men of the writing world.

Thinking about writing your book as running a marathon doesn't feel quite as charming as that image you had of popping out a cute little hard-bound baby, does it? I think the image helps, though. It keeps you honest with yourself. If you acknowledge that what you're doing, and what you intend to keep on doing, is hard work, you won't be so shocked when, thirty pages or a hundred pages or two hundred pages in, writing the novel stops being unalloyed fun and starts hurting. You hit walls with writing, the same way marathoners hit walls in their running. You exhaust the inspiration that got you through the first part, and you're nowhere near enough to the finish line to find any comfort or encouragement there. You have a hundred or so pages behind you and four-hundred or so pages ahead of you, and all of a sudden you realize that somebody stuck a hill in the middle of your track. And it goes up, not down.

So what you need to hear now is that after a little bit the adrenaline kicks in and you get your second wind, right? That the hill turns out to be an illusion. That it gets easier.

Bad news. There ain't no second wind; the hill is real; nothing ever gets easier. Completing a novel is hard. Really hard. As hard as running a marathon. You're impressed with the people you know who have completed marathons, whether or not their times were any good? You should have the same admiration for the folks you know who have completed novels, whether or not those books have sold. Even crappy novels require a faith and a dedication and a commitment that says good things about the folks who wrote them.

What gets you (or any writer) to the end of the book is not inspiration, or second wind, or a visit from the Book Fairy. It's process — and dogged, unswerving, stubborn commitment to process. It's promising yourself that you are going to write every day, by God, whether you feel like it or not. And it's keeping that promise when you don't feel like it. It's doing ten pages a day on the days that you can, and at least one page a day on the days when you think you can't do any. It's putting bad words on paper if you don't have any other words, just to meet your goals and keep your promise to yourself. It's trusting that better words will come, even if only in the rewrites.

It is accepting that writing a book is not about finishing the thing and sticking it in the mail, because that happens only rarely, and lasts for only a moment. Writing a book is no more about typing THE END than running a marathon is about crossing the finish line. Running the marathon is about picking up your feet and putting them down, one step at a time, for twenty-six miles — every one of those steps is exactly as valuable as every other one. Writing the novel is about filling five hundred double-spaced pages, one word at a time, day after day, until it's done. And every single word matters.

When it's done, you don't have an infant to love and gush and coo over. You have a piece of work that will require fixing — demanding more words, more pages, more patience. But you also have an achievement that you and you alone can claim. The woman who gives birth to a baby can claim credit all she wants, but you know and I know and she knows that she didn't make that baby. It grew without any input from her, and she can no more change the color of his eyes or the curve of his smile than she can give him wings and make him fly.

You, on the other hand, made your book. You built it one word at a time, and you can take credit for every cell and molecule and atom of its existence. You and you alone gave it life, and you did it the hard way.

One word at a time, plodding up the hill, going on because you promised yourself you would.

One word at a time. Process. Promises. Commitment.

When you finished it, you earned the right to be proud. And you probably were. Until you got an idea for another one. Writing books is like running marathons in another way, too. It's addictive. You crave the challenge after a while. You crave the "writers' high" that you get on those days when the pages flow from your fingertips. And you crave the pleasure that comes from knowing that you can do something most people only dream of doing.

So go write. You aren't hatching a baby. You're building your own trophy. And you can make it exactly the way you want it. "This is mine," you'll say. And you will have earned the right.

EXERCISE: Answer the following question in between 100 and 250 words:

What did you imagine the process of writing a book would be like, what do you think it will be like now, and how does that make you look at writing differently?

Say What You Mean

You want to talk about fear? This is where the process of writing comes right down to sweat under the armpits, racing pulse, dry mouth, and the urge to get up and go to the bathroom, or to switch over from the word processor to Maxis "Space Cadet" for five or ten quick games of pinball, or where the dust on the ceiling suddenly becomes an unbearable affront that you have to get rid of *Right Now*.

This is where facing anything else becomes preferable to facing the words on the page, because the words on the page are about to get up and bite you on the nose.

You are faced with uncomfortable truth and the urge to pussyfoot around an issue, and you have to decide which way you want to go — be honest, or whitewash. Here's my advice.

Say what you mean.

Euwww. It has all the appeal of picking your nose in public.

Writers live in abject terror of saying what they really mean, of being clearly and absolutely understood, of having no room in which they can back and fill and say, "You aren't seeing that the way I wrote it." They will, under most circumstances, choose to waffle, to squirm, to take the easy way out.

Don't believe me?

Look briefly at a pervasive, now-classic example of writers who, when faced with saying what they meant, chickened out. When Princess Diana died in a car crash, no matter how hard you avoided the news and current events, or how much you detested the sort of celebrity gossip that pervades common culture, you heard about this. Writers got more lines out of her death than they got out of anything since the assassination of John F. Kennedy. But in all those lines of print, in all those reams of notes read on-air, how many times did you hear or read that Diana 'died?'

Think about this for a second. I heard that she 'passed' and that 'she's left us' and that she's 'gone.' I heard of 'her tragedy' and 'her spirit living on' and a handful of other euphemisms. But for the life of me, I can't recall a single instance, outside of comedians making jokes about the whole thing, where someone said, "She's dead."

Well, death is one of those uncomfortable subjects, because we all know we're going to die, and none of us are too crazy about looking closely at the reality of the matter.

And Diana's death was unnerving.

She was young and rich and pretty and famous and that didn't save her. She went into a wall in a car while not wearing her seat belt and she died, just like poor commoners do, thus proving that nobody gets out of this alive. So you can almost (not quite, but almost) excuse the nervous tap dancing of the writers who took on her death and crapped out.

But not quite. After all, they did crap out. They didn't say what they meant.

Usually it isn't a matter of life or death, though, is it?

Let's say we're talking about you.

You're working on your book, and one of the characters is loosely based on your Aunt Bertie, who besides being fat and obnoxious also happens to be an alcoholic lesbian, and she makes a great character in a book except that you know damn well if she ever reads what you've written, she's going to know you were writing about her, and she's going to be pissed.

And what about the readers who object to your use of the word 'fat?' Never mind that Aunt Bertie weighs a bit over four hundred pounds and she does NOT have a glandular problem — you are going to have readers tell you that you shouldn't have called her 'fat.' Differently sized, maybe.

And that lesbian thing — she calls herself a dyke, but when you call her a dyke in the book, you can hear the chainsaws revving up. 'Dyke' is a word that you can't use unless you are one, isn't it?

So now you have some hard choices to make, and they aren't life or death, but what you decide is going to determine whether you have a story with meat on its bones or something that won't offend anybody, but won't tell any truths, either.

I'm sitting here right now, and my heart is pounding, because I know that what I am going to say is going to anger some of you. And I also know I'm going to say it anyway, because it's important, and you need to hear it.

You especially need to hear it if you think that 'differently abled' is an appropriate synonym for 'crippled,' or that 'appearance-challenged' is a better use of the English language than 'ugly.' Or if you buy into the nonsense that 'herstory' is a correct noun for 'revisionist history where women are the heroes.'

We are not all the same on this planet, folks. We are not actually black or white or red or yellow — we are in fact various shades of brown, and genetically we are closer to each other than a bunch of over-bred Cocker spaniels at an AKC show. But we are not all the same.

We are fat and thin and skinny; we are smart and stupid, geniuses and retards; we are straight and queer and everything in between; we are sick and healthy; we are tall and short; we are moral and immoral, good and evil; we are honest and we are liars.

We come in two sexes, male and female, and no matter what current Women's Studies classes say, women are not inherently better or purer or more noble than men; and no matter what the old guard at the country club says, men are not inherently better or purer or more capable than women. Some women are smarter than some men, some men are smarter than some women, and screwing around with the English language to censor any admission of this fact is not going to change the fact.

Nor is it going to change the fact that Aunt Bertie is fat and stinks of sweat even on cool days, or that she's a rude, self-centered, demanding woman who thinks the world owes her something because she's a lesbian.

She is who she is — a person and an individual. She is not a member of a class, nor is she an archetype or a symbol, and you can't compare her to any other people you know. She is who she is. And if you try to sugar-coat her to keep from offending people who are looking for the chance to be offended, you are going to end up eviscerating everything about her that makes her interesting.

Say what you mean.

Weasel words are for cowards.

They are for people who cannot face up to the fact that life is not fair, and is never going to be fair.

Weasel words are for people who want to tell everyone else what they can and cannot think, on the theory that if these weasel-writers can just control all those evil, smelly thoughts, the world will turn into a peaceful, matriarchal or patriarchal, gentle place where everyone is the same as everyone else — colorless, genderless, sexless, passive, obedient, inoffensive. The theory here is that if you call the turd floating in the toilet bowl 'feces' instead of 'shit', it will not stink.

I'm here to tell you that shit stinks, no matter what you call it, and if you genuinely believe that different words are going to change that fact, you need to have your head examined.

I'm here to tell you that men are different from women, and that those differences are both normal and good. Men are shot full of testosterone, and while that testosterone gives men a push toward aggressiveness, that aggressiveness is the thing that men channel into the creative drives that have given us some of the world's best architecture and literature and art, and that have created in men a sense of honor and passion and courage.

Women are shot full of estrogen, and while that estrogen push can make us bitchy as hell, it can also be channeled into creative drives that have given us some of the rest of the world's great literature and art, and have given birth to some great kids and some of the world's finest next generations. Motherhood is not a crime. Fatherhood is not a crime. Families are good things. Sex is pretty cool, parenthood is vital and — done well — both life-affirming and rewarding. Further, humanity is worth getting to know in the form that it takes. People **as**

they really are are fascinating, challenging, diverse, wonderful, awful, amazing, complex, many-faceted, colorful.

Don't castrate your writing or your characters because you're afraid to admit this, or afraid to face the nuts that come out of the woodwork when you say what you mean.

We as human beings are great and worth knowing and worth writing about **because** we are all different. That is the beauty of humanity — that we have risen above the inequalities and unfairnesses of life, and gone beyond our own weaknesses and handicaps and fears, and have made our stand based on who we are.

Not who we wished we were, not who the censors from all walks of life demanded that we pretend we were... but **who we are**.

Write the words that tell your story, even if they hurt.

Take a stand, knowing that the only way you are ever going to say something that matters is if you have the guts to say anything in the first place. Walk away from the weasel words, admit that death waits for you at the end of your life, call your character short or fat or skinny or stupid or ugly or perverted.

Tell the truth, even if it leaves you standing naked in front of everyone — clothes don't do anything but hide the truth of what's underneath them.

Say what you mean.

EXERCISE: Answer the following question in between 100 and 250 words:

What is the opinion you hold to be true that you hide from other people; why do you hide it; and how can you use this opinion in your fiction to make your book better?

The Writer's Toolbox

Every profession has its tools and requirements, and writing is no different. Hardware and software are nice, but they won't make you a writer. These four tools, used regularly and with the best of what you have in you, will.

- **English** — If you cannot spell, if you don't know how to punctuate a sentence, if you aren't sure about grammar, if you don't recognize the appropriate place to break a paragraph or remember how to set off dialogue from narrative, then stop right here. You must know all of these things so well that you don't have to think about them when you write. Your editor will not correct your awful spelling or sloppy punctuation; she will only reject your manuscript. Learn to use the written language first.

- **Persistence** — I could also call this "thick skin." You'll need it, whatever you choose to call it. You must accept that some of your work will not be good enough to sell, that some editors won't like your work even if it's good enough to sell, that things you send out will come back rejected. You must strive to improve constantly. You must realize that everything you write you could have written better, if only you'd known how … and then you must, on your next venture, figure out that 'how.' No writer, however good, is ever good enough.

- **Self-Confidence** — Conversely, you must believe that you have something to say, and that you alone are the best person in the world to say it. You must, on really lousy days, remember that you have a dream you are trying to make come true. You must have faith that what you want do do matters — that you are not just selling books (for if your only dream is to sell things, then you can sell shoes or TVs much more easily, and save a few trees in the process), but that you are reaching out to people, and trying, through your stories, to give them something they didn't have before.

- **Goals** — You must set them now, and set them high. Along with "write three pages a day" and "send off first story before next month" and "get paid for something I write," add "write a story that takes my own breath away" and "create a character so wonderful people write to you begging for more stories about him (or her)" and "include something so powerful in a novel that it changes someone's life for the better." Set small goals for your sanity…but large goals for your soul.

EXERCISE: Answer the following questions in between 100 and 250 words:

What is your strongest tool in the toolbox above, and how can you improve it?

What is your weakest tool in the toolbox above, and how can you improve it?

Finding Your Themes

Writing fiction is about telling stories...but what is telling stories about?

When you tell someone a story, why are you doing this? What compels you to create lies that have about them the ring of truth; what drives you to invent people and places and events and create a context that pulls them all together and makes them seem real?

When you're creating fiction, at heart you are searching for ways to create order in the universe.

You are digging into your core beliefs on how the world works, and running imaginary people through a trial universe built on these beliefs to see how both the people and the beliefs stand up under pressure. People who write fiction tend not to accept the world at face value — in general, they are the people who always got in trouble when they were little for asking "Why?" one time too many about something that, to everyone else, seemed pretty obvious.

When you started writing fiction, you probably did so at about the same time that you discovered that not only did your parents not have all the answers to the universe, but neither did anybody else. You discovered that, if you wanted an answer to that still-nagging "Why?" you were going to have to find the answer yourself.

Writing fiction is the act of questioning the silent, unanswering infinite and demanding that the infinite cough up a reply...and hurry up about it, too.

It is the ultimate defiance of that stock parental response, "Because I said so." Writing fiction is standing on the edge of the abyss of ignorance, looking across at the cliffs on the other side, and saying, "With nothing but words, I am going to build myself a bridge that takes me from here to there...and when I'm done, other people will be able to cross over that same bridge." It's an act of ultimate hubris, but of ultimate courage, too, because the abyss can eat you, and will if you slip.

So which bridges are worth building?

You can't cover the whole abyss. You can run a thousand lines from one side to the other if you live long enough, and you won't even cast a shadow on the voracious ignorance that lies beneath. All you can do is span the darkness with your slender threads, and build them strong enough that people can traverse them, and make them interesting enough that people will take the risk.

Which bridges are worth risking life and limb and hope and soul to create? Only those that take you to someplace you have not yet been.

And how do you decide which bridges those might be? You ask yourself the following question: To what questions in life have I not yet found a satisfactory answer?

These are some of my answers to that question:

Why do good things happen to bad people? Have you figured that one out yet? I haven't.

Why do bad things happen to good people? I've struggled with that one through a couple of books, and I have a couple of angles on it now, but certainly not the definitive one.

Why do we get old and die? Would living in these bodies forever be better? I've run with that one a couple of times now, too.

Why do we fall in love? Why do we fall out of love? Why do we hunger for the place that is just beyond the next horizon?

What is evil, and why do some people choose evil? What is good, and why do some people choose good? How are the first group of people different from the second group? How are they the same?

Is there a God, and if there is, does he or she know I'm here? And if he or she does...what is going on with my life?

Is there a heaven? Is there a hell? Is there anything that lies beyond the realm of this moment, this breath, this place and time? Do we have souls, and if so, what does that mean? Do we have a purpose for being here? What do we mean to each other? What constitutes living a meaningful life? What is love, and why does it matter?

These have all been my themes. Perhaps they are the same questions you have wondered about. Perhaps your curiosity and doubt run in completely different directions. In either case, your themes will define the power of your work, and its meaning not only to you but to everyone who reads it.

If you choose to work with safe themes — with questions to which you already know the answers — you'll write safe books.

You can have a very successful career writing safe books; after all, you won't drive too hard into the core of anyone's comfort zone, you won't force your readers to question the meaning of their own lives, you won't upset yourself or anyone else by reaching conclusions you don't like or find frightening.

But you won't grow as a writer, either, and you'll risk becoming bored with your characters and your stories and your work.

You can have a successful career writing about the questions you haven't answered, too. Mark Twain, my favorite writer, is also my favorite example of a man whose themes challenged the pat answers and asked the scary questions. He was a marvelous entertainer and a brilliant raconteur...but he also dared to look even God in the eye and say, "This doesn't make sense to me. Explain yourself."

In books and short stories and articles and essays and letters, again and again he held a mirror up to the world of his day and said, "Your actions belie your words, people. Your beliefs don't fit the facts. And your hypocrisy shames you...you deserve better of yourselves than to act the way you do." He wrote with everything he had. He dared the tough themes. And now, long after his death, when his colleagues who chose to write safely are nothing but footnotes in unread texts, Mark Twain continues to talk to us. His bridges across the abyss are still strong, still in use, still vital to those who want and need to get to the places he explored.

Every writer has something to say, but those writers whose works endure have dared to say something about the things that frighten them, confuse them, challenge them, and occasionally delight them.

They have not gone across the bridges built by others. They have dared to build their own.

You can find your own themes, and add power and depth to your work by daring to explore them through fiction. You can leave a worthwhile series of bridges into unknown territory, a solid series of roads away from ignorance and into knowledge that your readers can continue to use long after you are dust. In a world that cannot offer you physical immortality, you can leave something of your spirit, your courage, your hope and your integrity behind.

Find your themes — your REAL themes — and write them. I dare you.

EXERCISE: Answer the following question in between 100 and 250 words:

What are the things you have been afraid to write about, either because you do not know the answers or because you cannot believe the answers you know are the best ones available, and how can you write them?

Ten Steps to Finding Your Writing Voice

Your job as a writer is much more than just selling your books, believe it or not. Your job — if you want to make a living at this, anyway — is to sell yourself.

You are selling your unique perspective on life, your unique collection of beliefs, fears, hopes and dreams, your memories of childhood tribulation and triumphs and adult achievements and failures...your universe.

Anybody can sit down and write a story or a book — that is simply a matter of applying butt to chair and typing out three or four or ten pages a day until the thing is done. But not every book is salable, not every salable book will find an audience, and not every book that finds an audience will be able to bring the readers back for more of what the writer is selling.

Your goal is to achieve all three of those milestones:

1. *To sell your work;*

2. *To reach first-time readers with it;*

3. *To win these first-time readers over as repeat readers of your work.*

You do that by offering them something they can't get anywhere else — and the only thing in the universe that readers cannot get anywhere but from you is...you.

Which means you have to put yourself on your page. This is what is known in the writing business as developing your voice. Voice isn't merely style. Style would be easy by comparison. Style is watching your use of adjectives and doing a few flashy things with alliteration. Style without voice is hollow. Voice is style, plus theme, plus personal observations, plus passion, plus belief, plus desire. Voice is bleeding onto the page, and it can be a powerful, frightening, naked experience.

But your voice is your future in writing. And here is how you develop it.

1. Read everything.

You cannot be a successful writer if you don't read. That isn't opinion; that's fact. All writers read, and all good writers read a lot.

Read fiction, read nonfiction, read in the genre you love, read outside of it. Read WAY outside of it.

You cannot be a snob — don't write off any genre or type of book as being without redeeming qualities or lessons to teach you. The more you read, the more you will acquire a visceral instinct about what works for you, and an equally compelling instinct for what doesn't. You'll discover how stories are put together, get a feel for how good novels are paced and plotted and how bad ones fall apart, and you'll start developing a hunger to write specific stories, because you'll come across areas of fiction where nobody is writing the kind of books you want to read.

Reading is magic. It's your bread and butter. Don't neglect it.

2. Write everything.

Try your hand at non-fiction. Write romantic scenes. Put together a western character and run him through a fight scenario. Try fantasy, try SF, try romance, try mainstream. Write a sonnet, and some haiku, and a few limericks. Remember the first rule of writing:

Nothing you write is wasted.

Whether you use what you've produced or not, you will have learned from the experience…and you can never know too much. You might think you have the entire future of your writing planned out until you try your hand at something offbeat and discover that you can make that surprising subject sing. You might produce your first salable work completely outside of your previous area of specialization. (I wrote a handful of smartass SF sonnets as an exercise when I was first getting started, just to take a break from the hard SF that kept getting rejected — and out of the five I wrote in one day, I sold two. My first paid sales ever.)

3. Copy the best.

Do short exercises where you sit down and not only copy the style of your favorite writers, but also some of their themes and passions. Get as much into their heads as you can.

AND A LOUD ASIDE HERE: Do NOT copy their characters, their worlds, or their stories.

Don't plagiarize.

http://en.wikipedia.org/wiki/Plagiarism

Don't fanfic.

http://en.wikipedia.org/wiki/
Legal_issues_with_fan_fiction

Your objective in finding your own voice is to loosen up your writing muscles by writing your OWN work in someone else's voice, simply to shut up your inner critic.

When I was just getting started, I tried to write short stories and essays in Mark Twain's voice, but on subjects current at the time. I wrote sonnets that were deliberate takes on Shakespeare, but also on current subjects. "To An Android Lover" and "Ruminations on Impermanence in a Technophilic World," two of my sonnets, sold, demonstrating that these exercises can be profitable as well as fun.

They also let you get a feel for writing in a voice that you don't have to be responsible for — if you're writing as "Mark Twain," (or whoever your choice of writer will be) you'll be a lot less critical of yourself, and you'll free yourself up to experiment with content and structure in ways that you might resist when you're writing as yourself. After all, you have nothing to lose. If the stuff flops, it wasn't really you.

4. Play games.

Make endless lists — one-word lists of the things that excite you, the things that scare you, the things that you dream and fantasize about and hope for, the things you dread and fight to avoid. It is absolutely essential that these words have some special meaning to you — don't just go through a dictionary and pick them out randomly, or you'll find yourself staring at a blank page more often than not when trying to play the games that follow.

Great topics for lists are:

1. *Childhood memories.*
2. *Dreams and nightmares.*
3. *Ten gifts I'd give myself with magic.*
4. *If I could spend a million dollars, I'd buy…*
5. *What I want most in the world.*
6. *What I'd do anything to avoid.*
7. *Things that are creepy.*
8. *Things that are sexy.*
9. *Best foods.*
10. *Best times.*

You can come up with endless other topics for lists, too. Use these lists as triggers for writing games like the following:

- # "Three Words"
    Randomly choose one item from each of three lists. Use these words to create a title — you'll get something weird like "Lake Bones Ice Cream," or "Naked Broken-Glass Monkeys." Without allowing yourself to think about these words or censor what you're putting on the page, just start writing, letting the words conjure images and stories for you. Write for ten minutes without allowing yourself to stop or correct anything.

- **"Chasing Your Tail"**

    Start with a random word on one of your lists. Write for two or three minutes on that word, not allowing yourself to stop writing, to back up, or to correct. Immediately choose by random means a second word from any one of your lists. Start writing again, connecting this word to what you were writing about before. Write for two or three minutes; then pick another word which you connect to the subject you've been writing about with the first two. Run with this pattern of choosing and following for as long as you wish, or can.

- **"Theme"**

    Randomly choose only one word, and write for ten minutes on just that word, exploring everything about it that matters to you, why the subject is compelling to you, what memories it stirs in you, what hopes or fears it shakes loose in you, places, sounds, scents and tastes that appear as you're writing. Don't censor, don't stop writing for any reason, don't correct.

Again, you can come up with endless variations on these games that you can play by yourself or with other writers in writers' groups. The idea is to dig beneath your surface and start freeing up things that you have kept hidden even from yourself.

5. Challenge your preconceptions.

You don't know everything about yourself. You only think you do. The more you trust yourself to write without correction, the more you'll discover that you're a lot deeper and more interesting and more complex than you imagined.

But you'll find out a lot about yourself by pushing some of your own buttons, too, and I recommend that from time to time you do. If you're a staunch Republican, write an essay from inside the head of a liberal Democrat who is in favor of the thing you most despise, whether it is entitlement spending or gun control or free abortions on demand. If you're strongly science-oriented, write from inside the head of a modern mystic who makes a living as a professional psychic, and who strongly and passionately believes in his or her work. If you're strongly religiously oriented, write from inside the head of a person who loathes all religion, and has good reason for doing so.

Your job in this exercise is to **become**, although only temporarily, the thing that most frightens, angers, or bewilders you. To do it right, you have to allow your enemy to convince you of his rightness — you cannot allow yourself to convince him. For example, the strongly Christian writer cannot have the character he is writing experience a conversion to Christianity or see the error of his ways — he must, instead, have the agnostic present his logic so well that at the end of the argument, the agnostic remains firmly convinced he is right.

I'll tell you right now that this is some of the toughest writing that you'll ever do. Don't try it when you're tired or cranky or when you have a headache — you'll probably get one from this particular exercise even if you felt great beforehand. But do take the leap and do this. It is the absolute best way (if you play fairly) that I've ever found to start developing characters that aren't either transparent versions of yourself or pathetically weak straw men that you can triumph over as villains.

6. Dare to be dreadful.

When you're finding your voice, you're going to be doing a lot of experimenting. Some of what you write, frankly, is going to be lousy. Some of it will shock you with how good you really are. But the only way you'll get any of the good stuff is if you allow yourself to put whatever comes into your head down on the page without demanding salable prose of yourself.

This isn't the time to be shooting for commercial viability. When your internal editor switches on, hit him over the head with a frying pan, preferably a cast iron one.

7. Write from passion.

If you don't care about the things you're writing about, you will **never** discover your true voice. Your voice does not exist when you're trying to write a book in a genre you hate because you think it will be an easy way to make a quick buck. Your voice does not exist in the thin and cheap places of your heart or the shallow end of your soul. Voice lives in the deep waters and the dark places of your soul, and it will only venture out when you make sure you've given it space to move and room to breathe.

8. Take risks.

Choose to write about themes that your internal editor insists are too dangerous, too controversial, too embarrassing to be put on the paper. Imagine that your mom (or your other toughest critic) is looking over your shoulder with a raised eyebrow and a prudish expression on her face. Now shock her.

9. Remember that complacency is your worst enemy.

If you're comfortable, if you're rolling along without having to really think, if you haven't had to challenge yourself, if you know that everyone is going to approve of what you've done — you're wasting your time. Writing done from a position of comfort will never say anything worthwhile.

10. Remember that fear is your best friend.

If your heart is beating fast and your palms are sweating and your mouth is dry, you're writing from the part of yourself that has something to say that will be worth hearing. Persevere. I've never written anything that I've really loved that didn't have me, during many portions of the manuscript, on the edge of my seat from nerves, certain that I couldn't carry off what I was trying to do, certain that if I did I would so embarrass myself that I'd never be able to show my face in public again — and I kept writing anyway.

At the heart of everything that you've ever read that moved you, touched you, changed your life, there was a writer's fear. And a writer's determination to say what he had to say in spite of that fear.

So be afraid. Be very afraid. And then thank your fear for telling you that what you're doing, you're doing right.

Voice is born from a lot of words and a lot of work — but not just any words or any work will do. You have to bleed a little. You have to shiver a little. You have to love a lot — love your writing, love your failures, love your courage in going on in spite of them, love every small triumph that points toward eventual success.

You already have a voice.

It's beautiful, it's unique, it's the voice of a best-seller. Your job is to lead it from the darkest of the dark places and the deepest of the deep waters into the light of day.

EXERCISE: Answer the following question in between 100 and 250 words, then do the additional exercise:

Who is your favorite writer, and what could you write in his or her voice about one of the things you're afraid to say in your own voice? (Look back to your previous exercises for ideas)?

Do that now.

How to Finish a Novel

The problem with novels is that you can't sit down in one day and complete one from start to finish. (At least I can't. If you can, you have my undying envy.) Novels are long. Generally, a salable length is between 90,000 and 150,000 words...and that, fellow writer, is a lot of words.

Quality self-pubbed novels seem to start at around 50,000 to 60,000 words, and the top limit is whatever the author decides. Part of why self-pub is so very cool.

So how do you get from "Once upon a time...." to "THE END"?

These are the techniques that have worked for me.

First, know how it ends.

This may seem obvious — but then again, maybe not. Back in my days of thirty-page novel starts that never went anywhere, I never knew how the story would end. It was only when I figured this key point out that I finished a novel. (**Hearts in Stitches**, a supposed-to-be funny romance novel about a nurse and an architect that, fortunately, died by fire. Actually, was **killed** by fire. By me. On purpose. Trust me — it was kinder that way.)

You can simply tell yourself, "When I reach the part of this story, the heroine kills the villain with his own sword just as he's about to kill her in front of the bound hero, and then the heroine frees the hero and they both escape from the burning building." You can hold that in your head and work with it, and it may be enough.

If it isn't, go to the next step.

Write your ending, and then write to it.

You may discover, on thinking about your ending, that you can't quite get all the little ins and outs of that climactic scene or series of scenes clear in your head. There may be a lot happening — it can be very tough to keep multiple threads in a complex story straight.

If this is the case, as it often is for me, write the last scene or couple of scenes, or the big climax scene, if you're going to do a bit of wrapping up after that's finished. Pretend the entire rest of the book is done, pretend that everything is already in place, and just start writing.

When you do this, you'll probably discover that there are things you're going to have to put in place earlier in the book so that you can have them available to use during the climax. You know how all those carefully hidden clues in mystery novels suddenly reveal themselves in the last scene, and you smack yourself on the head and say, "I should have seen that coming — how did the writer **do** that so cleverly?" Well, this is how. The writer wrote the ending, then filled up the middle with all the stuff he'd already used, disguising it and throwing red herrings around it so that you wouldn't catch on.

Neat, huh?

But maybe you're having trouble bridging the vast gap between your hot beginning and that elusive end. If so, here's the first way you can get through the middle.

Create five or six "candy-bar" scenes, and use them to keep you moving forward.

First, let me define a "candy-bar" scene. It's one that you're just itching to write — something sweet enough that you can dangle it on a stick in front of yourself so that you can say, "When I've done these next three chapters, I'll get to write **that** one.

If you're doing fantasy, maybe one of your candy-bar scenes will be the one where the hero discovers for the first time that he can control some magical force or element...but that he can't yet control it very well. You can just imagine the trouble you're going to cause for him, and how much fun you're going to have causing it.

If you're writing mainstream, maybe the thing you're most itching to put on paper is the moment when your main character discovers that she isn't alone in the world — that somewhere out there, she has a half-sister...and now all she has to do is find her.

If you're writing romance, maybe the hot-and-heavy scenes are the ones you can use for candy-bars. (Or maybe not. Every time I write a sex scene, I feel like my mother is looking over my shoulder, saying, "And just where did you learn **that**?")

Make sure your candy-bar scenes are spread out through the book, not all clumped together. Write down a single sentence for each of them. Don't allow yourself to do more than that, or you'll lose the impetus to move through the intervening scenes.

Even if you have your ending in place and great candy-bar scenes to lure yourself onward, though, there are things that can keep you from finishing. If you're still having trouble, check out these next few suggestions and see if any bells start ringing.

Write about people you enjoy spending time with.

This isn't the same as writing about people you like. You can really hate some of your characters, but still enjoy spending time with them, simply because what they do is so interesting. You don't use the same criteria for picking story characters that you do for picking friends. But if, every time one of your main characters walks onto the page, your first thought is, "Oh, God — that old bore," it's time to rethink your cast list. Kill him, improve him...or just erase him.

Use an outline.

This is, I know, anathema to many writers. Some believe it makes the process of writing mechanical. Some think it removes the element of discovery from the writing process.

But I've been using outlines since I started. I've only written one book without one (**Sympathy for the Devil**) and I haven't found outlines at all restraining. Remember that an outline is only a map. If you find some unmarked side roads you want to explore once you're moving well, explore them. If you discover an entirely different route than the one you mapped out, take it. My finished books only bear passing resemblance to the outlines that spawned them...but the outline allows me to check from time to time to make sure my new route will still get me to my chosen destination.

(And I don't do standard outlines, either. Re-read the Notecarding chapter from the **Practice: The Workshops** section if you forget how to do a light, effective index card outline.)

Allow yourself to be surprised.

This is for the other half of the writing universe — the half that sticks rigidly to the outline, that takes characters who go off in their own directions as a personal affront, and that feels that the writer must control the story at all times.

Breathe, guys.

Control is seriously overrated. Take this from the person who used to write thirty-page chapters. Not twenty-nine. Not thirty-one. Thirty. Every chapter. I was proud of the fact that I could write a story that would have the exact word count called for in the contract.

Life is too short for that sort of nonsense. And when you're writing, why put yourself on a Procrustean bed and whack off your own feet, just to maintain your rigid sense of control? If your subconscious mind is taking your character in a new direction — it's still you. You're still the writer. You can stop the process at any time. But if you don't ever let yourself go off on tangents, you'll never discover the amazing secrets you've been hiding from yourself.

And your writing will be dry and forced, and you may discover that you have less and less reason to finish each book, because you know there will be no surprises.

Write because you want to, not because you should.

Nobody **should** write a book. If writing isn't something you're doing because you love it, don't do it, because it isn't a quick way to riches and it isn't a quick way to fame. It's hard work — the thing you might be finding out when you're sitting down to try to finish your book and hitting the invisible wall.

Further, there is nothing in your head that you *owe* the world. What you have inside your skull is your own private property, beholden to no one. If you want to put it into books, great. But if you think you have some sort of duty to do this, I'm going to set you free. You don't owe anybody on this planet your thoughts, no matter how wonderful they may be.

If you don't LIKE to write, don't.

Write what you love, not "what sells."

Back to **Hearts in Stitches**, the one romance novel*· I tried. I had this vision of myself as a romance novelist, putting out one book every two months and sitting on a bank account that would shame Fort Knox. The problem with this lovely image is that I was writing romance not because it was what I loved with a passion, but because I didn't mind romances, and some of them I thought were kind of cute, and I thought they'd be an easy way to make a buck. Here's a little lesson I learned from that experiment — there is no harder money to make than "easy money." I had to beat myself with a baseball bat to finish that book, and when it was done, it wasn't very good. It was competent — I got personal rejections with comments from each place I sent it — but it lacked heart and soul.

When I moved into SF and fantasy and started writing what I loved simply because I loved it, I started selling. I sold the first book I wrote to the first place I sent it. Which isn't a guarantee that you will do the same. You won't have to hurt yourself to finish your books if you're doing what you love, though. *What you will not do for love, you should not do for money.*

And that's my take on getting from the beginning of your novel to the end. I hope these tips point you in the right direction and make the experience fun and exciting for you.

EXERCISE: Answer the following question in between 100 and 250 words:

What do you love enough to pursue it for a hundred thousand words, and why do you love it?

An addendum, written some years after this article: Thanks to a friend with a vast reading knowledge of the romance field, I discovered romance novels that I did love — some paranormals, some romantic suspense thrillers — and I have come full circle. I wrote four paranormal suspense novels that received all sorts of critical recognition — and since the rights have reverted to me, I'm self-publishing them.

Never say never. You can discover things to stir your passion in places you thought you already looked.

How to Collaborate, And How Not To

Collaborations are the proverbial double-edged sword — they can hurt you even as they help you. They're fun to do, but they're harder to sell than solo novels.

If you get one with a big-name author and no one has ever heard of you, the chances are the book will sell pretty well and you'll make some money, but you'll do ninety percent of the work and even though a lot of people will read the book, no one will know who you are.

If you get one and you *are* the big-name author, the collaboration won't sell as well as your regular work, you'll do ninety percent of the work, and the few of your regular fans who read the book will complain that it isn't much like your usual work.

If you and your buddy are doing one together, you'll do ninety percent of the work, and he'll do ninety percent of the work because you'll each be adding to, subtracting from, and altering the work the other writer did in order to get the pieces to fit.

And now the careful readers and the math whizzes among you will be saying, "If Collaborator A and and Collaborator B each do ninety percent of the work, that's one-hundred eighty percent. That doesn't add up."

Unfortunately it does. Collaborations are much more work than solo novels. They can be much more frustrating. They present special legal problems. They can cost you in a lot of hidden ways.

And you're saying, "Yes, but my friend and I have this idea and we still want to do a collaboration."

All right. If you're going to do one, here are the things that I've learned that can help you, and the things I've found out the hard way can hurt you.

Always determine in advance who will do what and who will own what. And put down your agreements in writing.

Now **you're** going to say, "Okay, that one doesn't apply to me because I'm going to be doing **my** collaboration with my best friend. Next!"

Wait. Please. This is the most important thing that you can do, right now, to make sure that you and your friend are still friends after the collaboration is done. I lost a friend — a good friend — over a collaboration, and I might have lost her anyway, but if we had written down, in advance, what each of us would be required to do to complete an acceptable collaboration, maybe we wouldn't have ended up never speaking to each other again.

Here are the absolute minimum number of things you need to agree on, in writing, before you start your project.

- Who owns each character and the universe you have created (or each part of it), and whether either of you has the right to do solo works in the universe or whether it can only be used for collaborative ventures.

- What each of you may and may not do to characters owned by the other.

- Who gets final edit on the manuscript or manuscripts, or if this will change from book to book, how you will determine in advance who will get final edit each time. (And I'm telling you right now, you cannot both have final edit. Only one person can ever have the last word. Figure out before you type the first word who that person is going to be.)

- How you will divide the work itself.

- What will happen to the universe and its characters if one or both of you want to drop out.

- How you will resolve differences if one of you does work that the other deems unacceptable, inappropriate, or simply wrong for the world.

- Whose name will go first on the cover. It's going to have to be the same one every time, so figure it out now.

There is a further list of things that you'll need to work out in advance if one or both of you have already sold solo works, or has an agent and/or a publisher.

- Whose agent or agency will negotiate contracts and subrights.

- Who will deal primarily with the editor.

- Who will write outlines and treatments.

- How the money will be divided in both best- and worst-case situations, and who will be the one who receives payment and will be responsible for paying the other one.

An agent can help you with some of this stuff, but some of it you're going to have to figure out on your own. It isn't fun. It is important.

If you're like most potential collaborators, this little list has startled you. None of us, when we're sitting down with a friend hammering out story concepts and shaping our universe and characters together, is thinking, "Now who's going to get first billing on the book and who is going to edit whom, and what happens if my friend turns out not to be able to finish his half of the work so that I get stuck doing all of it?"

We're just having fun, playing around with the magic of creation, and all the things that can and eventually will go wrong are still a million miles away. Please believe me when I tell you that all the best intentions in the world won't help you when things start going wrong. *Then* you need to have things in writing, and you need to have had them in writing from the start.

Write a good outline and stick with it.

This doesn't seem like such a big deal. You and your friend share a vision. You've talked endlessly about it, you know who your characters are and where you want them to go, and the fact that you don't have the whole story worked out doesn't seem relevant.

Divide your workload clearly.

If one of you is going to do the even chapters and the other one is going to do the odds, fine. If one is going to do all the scenes with Elmira Fairclothe and the other is going to write only from the point of view of Studly Stallionbritches, that's okay too. If you want to write the first draft and have your friend do the second, that also works.

What you **don't** want is to be bopping along on chapter three and have your collaborator suddenly start having ducks because you've stepped on what he saw as his territory. Nor do you want to have your collaborator complain that you're a lazy slob who's not holding up your end of the workload.

Figure out why you want to do a collaboration in the first place, and both of you sit down and work out what each of you contributes.

The ideal collaboration is one in which the book you are writing together is one neither of you could write alone. If one of you is a brilliant mathematician and the other is a professional-caliber sculptor and you're doing a book on the mathematics of sculpture, you're heading in the right direction. If one of you has vast knowledge of military history and the other is equally proficient in all things magical and fantastical and you're developing a huge fantasy series that involves magical battles with well-thought-out tactics and strategy, you're right on the money.

If, however, both of you are doing this because you think it will be easier than writing a whole book by yourself, go home, go to bed, and stay there until you come to your senses. Good collaborations are not simply as hard as solo novels; they aren't even merely twice as hard to write as good solo novels. They are harder by a full order of magnitude.

Remember your priorities.

This can be tough once you're well into the project, when it stops being one big hoot and starts feeling like real work. So give some thought to the question while you're still having lots of fun. Was your goal just to do a fun story with your friend? Was it to get both of you published? Was it to make both of you financially independent? (Good luck if that's the case — collaborations are not usually the golden road to riches.) Or were you aiming for something else? And what is going to satisfy both of you? Just completing a whole book? Selling it? Still being friends once it's done?

However — from my own experience here — the act of writing changes the vision, and even **with** an outline you can end up in trouble. My friend and I had agreed to write a book together in a universe that I created in which the heroine was so strong in her faith and her love of her fellow humans that she transformed and redeemed the fallen angel who was sent to lead her astray. It was supposed to be both a life-affirming and a funny book, the start of a series of collaborative books in which humans would interact with denizens from Hell and Heaven, and in which God would demonstrate a seriously warped sense of humor. I wrote the outline, she was to do the first draft, I was to do the final draft.

Somewhere along the way, she veered seriously from the outline. What had started out a fun and funny book turned very dark, ending with the heroine seduced away from her faith, left hopeless and broken and bound for Hell, with the fallen angel triumphant.

When I got her manuscript, I had a problem. As she'd written it, the story no longer set up the second, third, and fourth books, which I'd sold at the same time with three other writers, all of whom were already working on their books. I tried to rewrite it, but I couldn't. It was too far from what I had to have, in both tone and content.

I ended up sending it back to her with a long letter explaining why I couldn't use it — I wrote a completely different solo book in just under a month to meet the deadline, an exhausting experience in itself, but made worse because my friend was deeply hurt that I'd rejected her book, deeply hurt that I had written a letter to her explaining my decisions instead of telling her in person (a piece of sheer stupidity on my part — my publisher told me to give her the news in writing and instead of treating her like a friend I did as he suggested and treated her as any other business associate), and just plain hurt because. She never spoke to me again, and I'll tell you, no book is worth a friend.

The deal is different for two established pros working together than it is for two beginners. Agents frequently introduce potential collaborators — you frequently meet the person you're going to be working with for the first time after you've already signed the contract (though you both will have done a fair amount of prep work before.)

You don't have emotion or the potential loss of friendship riding on your project if it fails. Usually both of you already have a pretty good idea of how the business works. It's less exciting, but you have less to lose — and you can make some good friends if you and your collaborators get on well.

If you've gone through this list and you know how you want to divvy up the work and you've covered all your potential trouble spots and worked them out in advance and you still want to do the collaboration, you should do fine.

Remember that joint projects always take longer than you planned, always contain some surprises, and rarely go turn out the way you expected. They can be fun if you if you know this in advance and have already made allowances.

EXERCISE: Answer the following question in between 100 and 250 words:

Write out what will happen to your world and characters if you and your collaborator stop working together, and then ask yourself if you could have as much fun working in a world you owned completely.

How to Query an Agent or Editor

I received a letter recently asking if it would be better to send a humorous letter to an agent when asking for representation than a more serious one. I've included my response below, along with a sample query letter and suggestions that you might find helpful if you've reached this stage.

My reply:

> *There is no secret to getting an agent but persistence, sadly. I wouldn't recommend a gimmick or a "funny" letter. Every agent and editor and publisher I know is inundated by people trying to be different, when what all of them desperately want is someone who is professional. I would recommend including a one-page single-spaced synopsis of the work you're hoping to have the agent submit that tells the complete story, including the ending. I would keep the letter as businesslike and short as possible.*

About persistence — when I finished *Fire in the Mist*, I queried Russ Galen. He turned me down by form letter, but I was determined that he was going to be my agent (he was one of the best in the field). I didn't bother querying anyone else, because I didn't want anyone else. So I sold my first novel on my own, and when I did, wrote him a note that said, basically, "You suggested that I query you again once I sold something. I sold my first book the first time out to the first place I sent it, within a month of sending it out. Would you be interested in representing me now?"

He contacted me by phone the day he got the letter.

That's the hard way to get an agent, kind of like drawing a spades royal flush in a game of five card draw with nothing wild.

But there isn't an easy way. There will only be your way, and the way of the other few who persist until they succeed.

Here's a sample of what you say in a query letter to an agent:

```
Joe Writer

Address
Address
Phone Number
email@emailaddress.com

Date

Agent Name-spelled-right
Brilliant Literary Agency
Address
Address

Dear Agent Name-spelled-right,

In 3110 AD, three battered space fighter
pilots, cut off from their home ship and
nearly out of ammo and air, take refuge on a
tiny moon — and there discover the key to
their alien enemies' destruction, a key that
will save humanity if only they can survive to
get their discovery home.

DAGGER MOON, 90,000 words, is my first novel.
I've enclosed a single-page synopsis of the
story. The novel is complete should you decide
you would like to see more. You'll find my
SASE enclosed.

Thank you for your time. I eagerly await your
response.

All my best wishes,

Joe Writer
```

Pointers:

- **Be specific.** Know exactly what you've written, and describe it by its genre. Time-travel romance, mainstream thriller, high fantasy trilogy (NOTE — If you've written a book that will require more than one volume to tell the story, and have no track record with an agent or publisher, you need to have the complete story finished before you send it off, no matter how many volumes it takes. Single-volume works are easier for a beginner to sell. There are exceptions. If you're Robert Jordan or J. V. Jones, you might be one of them. But if you aren't, my advice stands.)

- **Be polite.** You are asking for someone to invest his time in reading your work. You are **asking a favor of a stranger.** PLEASE keep this in mind. You are not yet in the position to grant favors, and comments implying that you are — for example, "You are one of the lucky few to whom I'm offering the chance to represent me." — will only get your letter dumped in the trash.

- **Be modest.** Don't say your manuscript is the best book ever written, or that it will make a million dollars, or that you are the next William Shakespeare. Let your work speak for yourself. If you're any good, the agent will figure that out by reading what you've written. If you try to tell him how great you are, you'll just come off looking like a boor and an idiot.

- **Be reasonable.** Don't demand that he represent you, or threaten to kill yourself if he doesn't. Don't offer bribes. Don't write on pink stationery with purple ink. Don't send your entire manuscript unasked. Put yourself in the agent's place. Imagine that you got dozens of letters a day from complete strangers who all wanted you to do things for them. Imagine that most of the requests had no merit, that most of the people were rude, and that most of the work they sent you was anywhere from mediocre to downright awful. Imagine getting one polite, intelligent, businesslike letter in the midst of all that chaos. Now — be the writer of **that** letter.

The Internet and self-publishing have changed the process of querying — it's no longer dependent upon high-rag-content 24-pound-bond paper and a fresh typewriter ribbon.

Some agents accept e-mails. Some don't. Same with editors.

If you want to go with commercial rather than self-publishing, use the Internet to research the agents or editors you want to work with, and find out their preferences **before** you query.

SECTION IV
Frequently Asked Questions

I get a lot of mail — mostly e-mail these days. A lot of that mail comes in from writers who have questions.

And the questions that come up the most frequently, I've answered on my website on my FAQs pages.

These are updated versions of the most important of those pages, revised to include self-publishing where it's relevant, as well as to include the Self-Publishing FAQ, wherein a quarter century's worth of frustration at the whole commercial publishing process managed, I'm afraid, to leak out. Just a bit.

These are timely as I write this, in 2012. But the state of publishing is chaotic right now, and I have no idea how things will change in the next few years. Except I predict they'll change quickly.

If you want to write for a living, start scouring the Internet for current changes in publishing and distribution, contracts, royalties, indie publishing, and much more now. Don't get left behind.

The FAQs (Frequently Asked Questions) About Self-Publishing

On many of the articles on your website, you come down hard on self-publishing. What's up with that?

I wrote some of the articles now published on HollyLisle.com back in the late 1980s, as part of a print newsletter I did for my writer's group.

Some of the articles on the site I wrote in the 1990s and 2000s before 2011, when Commercial Publishing was the only respectable game in town, and its Evil Alternative was Vanity Publishing (also known as "The Writer Gets Screwed" publishing). Both commercial publishing and vanity publishing are still around.

The new kid in town, however — *Self-Publishing With Really Cool Sharp Pointy Teeth* — did not yet exist, and agents, editors, and publishers of both the Commercial and Vanity varieties had no clue it was coming.

I offered the best information available at the time, which was Go With Commercial Publishing because you don't want to get screwed by Evil Vanity Publishing. Which, on the Commercial FAQS, I call "self-publishing" because at the time, that WAS almost all self-publishing.

If you still want to publish your work The Way Our Forefathers Did (in the 1900s — prior to that, almost everyone, including my favorite writer, Mark Twain, self-published), then my information on Commercial Publishing stands as written. It's good info, it's true, and it will save you from getting screwed. All good things.

Just understand that *REAL Self-Publishing has now arrived*, and for writers who want to make a living at this, it is the Holy Grail within your reach, you can afford to do it right even if you're damn near penniless, and **if** you want to make your living as a full-time writer, you're nuts not to.

What is Commercial Publishing vs. Self-Publishing?

In Commercial Publishing, you go through the *Ritual of Self-Abasement and Desperation* until you are Anointed, you follow the *Path of Editor Supplication* until your book is properly sliced upon the *Procrustean Bed of the Least Common Denominator*, you write novels that rarely get great publisher support and that almost always get killed rapidly and brutally by chain bookstores and their retarded computerized ordering systems, and you grovel and weep when your publisher sings *The Ballad Of The Accountants of Mayhem Who Tell Us Your Books Did Not Do As Well As We Had Hoped* and tosses you out the door to find another publisher and start over.

Okay, that was unnecessarily smart-ass — but *like many writers who've sold more than thirty novels** via the commercial (mainstream, professional) publishing system, I have some deep and ugly scars to show for it, and I tend to get a little edgy. So let me try again.

Commercial (Mainstream, Professional) Publishing is the following process:

- Write a novel.

- Revise it to make it your best possible work.

- Send it to agents and editors until someone says "Yes, we want that,"… or until you grow old and die. (Dammit — drifted into smart-ass again there. Doesn't mean it's not true, but it ain't nice.)

- Sign a contract that allows the publishing house to keep almost all of the money the book will ever make in exchange for an advance and (usually mythical) twice-yearly royalties.

- Get an agent to make sure that this contract is as favorable to you as is humanly possible.

- Sign additional contracts for each subsequent book or series of books.

- Promote the hell out of your work, because unless you're a superstar, your publisher won't — even though your promotion will not add much (or anything) to your income.

- Get paid rarely, late, or not at all unless you hit the magic trifecta of a first-novel best-seller, increasing sales for each subsequent book, and every book enough like the others to keep your complete readership in one place without losing them to boredom (yours or theirs) or quality die-off of your novels.

- Watch your backlist go out of print so you will never have the chance of seeing royalties on older titles, or of building a readership based on your deep list of in-print books.

- Turn into a grumpy curmudgeon who tells new writers they'd be better off digging ditches for a living.

Okay. Clearly I've buried the needle on my Smart-Ass-O'-Meter for this particular topic, but I have done the Dance Of Publishing Pain, Numfar** — and I'm NOT going to tell you you'd be better off digging ditches for a living.

I'm going to tell you writing fiction is the best damn job on the planet.

But not if you're doing it the old-fashioned way. Not anymore.

This is the better way.

High-Quality Self-Publishing is the following process:

- Write a novel.

- Revise it to make it your best possible work.

- Hire a copyeditor to make sure the book is as error-free as humanly possible.

- Buy your ISBNs.

- Either package the book yourself for Kindle, Nook, iBooks, and other e-book sellers you may decide to use, or hire a packager to do this for you (some packagers provide cover art, copyediting, and other goodies for reasonable additional fees). LEGITIMATE book packagers will NOT claim any rights to your work, will NOT include **their** ISBNs on your work, and will not receive any compensation from your work — you will pay them to set up your book, and that's the only money they will ever see for each title they produce for you.

- Publish the book you wanted to write, not the book an editor looking at accounting numbers and spreadsheets thought you'd be better off writing.

- Promote your work, because it's your work, and you're the one who gets paid when you sell it.

- Get paid monthly, and as you add more books to your list, get paid monthly for them, too.

- Own a growing backlist of books that will never go out of print unless YOU choose to take them out of print.

Self-publishing well is a bit more work than Commercial publishing. And you have to know more things. You have to understand your rights. You have to get to know your readers. Personally — online is fine, though — you don't have to invite them to your house. You're sort of hoping once you get going on this, they wouldn't all fit.

You have to take initiative to get every part of the process done — and that can be hard, and you have to spend real money on your books to buy your ISBNs, and if you choose to hire someone to format your books or design your covers, you have to pay for that, too. You control these costs, though, and can do this on an incredibly thin shoestring if you need to.

And you'll never have an editor tell you, as one of mine told me, that writers should all have real jobs so they don't lose touch with the real world — and that she hoped I hadn't quit mine. (I'd been writing full-time for about seven years at that point.)

What is Vanity Publishing vs. Self-Publishing?

Vanity Publishing still exists, and you have to be very careful to stay far, far away from it.

- If you have to sign a contract that will give the publisher the right to sell your books and profit from them — but you are paying the publisher to create your books — you're vanity publishing.

- If your publisher owns the ISBN that goes on this book — and if you don't know who owns the ISBN for your book, your publisher does, because if you didn't buy it yourself and if you don't have the receipt in hand to prove it, someone else bought it and it belongs to them — you're vanity publishing.

- If you MUST publish your book on the site that formatted the book for you, or you are prohibited from publishing it to any other site you like (Kindle, iBooks, Nook, Smashwords, etc.) you are vanity publishing.

If you are truly self-publishing, you will own ALL your rights, you will own your ISBN, and you can publish the book anywhere and everywhere you want.

When would you recommend a writer self-publish?

There are two ways to take this question, and I'll answer both here.

The first version of this question is "When would you suggest the writer abandon the pursuit of Commercial Publishing to begin Self-Publishing?"

Well...

My inner smart-ass says: Yesterday?

My more professional other self notes that there are a few reasons to Commercial Publish.

- You want to see your books on bookshelves in Big Chain Bookstores (the ones that haven't yet gone under).

- You don't want to have to carry the full responsibility for the quality of your books and the promotion of your work. (Though publisher promotion is a myth for most books that get published, so don't get comfortable.)

- You want the very real legitimizing effect you'll get from having sold your work to Penguin Putnam, Tor, Baen, Scholastic, HarperCollins, Time-Warner, etc. (to name some of the publishers of my work). If you've published with the big boys, no one can ever say you're not a "real writer." And if you care what people think (family, friends, strangers, whatever...), you're going to have to do the Dance.

But if you want to:

- Build up a career that will let you live on your writing income;

- Keep your backlist in print;

- Write the books you want to write, and not the books publishing bean-counters think will sell;

- Connect with your readers directly, and know you're free to keep writing what they like;

- Own your own work, your own business and your own future...

...Then you want to self-publish. *First, not after publishers have tied up years worth of your work* while they publish it badly, promote it not at all, and never, ever send you money for what they do sell.

The second version of this question is, "When will I be ready to put my work out there?"

The answer to that one is, (as it is in the Commercial Publishing FAQ), **When your book is good enough.**

Only now, dammit, I can't default to the old Commercial Publishing answer of "you'll know it's good enough because it sells."

You need to know how to write well. Tell a good story. Revise your work.

It wouldn't hurt to have someone who has real professional qualifications as an editor dig into a manuscript and give it a deep, intense "here's what you did right, here's what you did wrong, and here's why" critique of your work. There are people you can pay to do this. The problem is that some of them are honest and legitimate, and some of them are scam artists, and I have no clue which are which.

I can teach you how to tell a good story and how to do professional revision on your work. HollyLisle.com is loaded with free articles and workshops, and if you're looking for in-depth step-by-step instruction on every aspect of writing professionally, I offer paid courses as well.

Here's the link:

http://howtothinksideways.com/writing-courses

My biggest courses include a private students-and-grads-only writers' community where you can meet other writers, trade crits, develop professional connections, and discover a multitude of skills and processes that will allow you to make your work publishable, and will give you connections to other folks who will not only read it and cheer you on, but help you promote it.

But to head off the question that does come, I will not read your work — not even if you offer to pay me. Not even if you offer to pay me a LOT (and I say this because there have been folks who raised the price offer to insane levels before finally believing me. This is not work I do, and I don't make exceptions.)

I make enough money to live on, so I don't have to take work that makes me unhappy. **I am only happy when I am creating;** editing and critting make me miserable beyond words. There are folks who love to edit and crit. It would be worth your while to find one of them who is both skilled and honest, and to pay him for his time.

Do you need an agent if you self-publish?

Depends. Mostly, no — but if you suddenly find yourself faced with an offer of movie rights, or a Commercial Publisher wants to buy print rights to your work, or, if anything else happens and you're interested in saying yes, but there are contracts involved, YOU NEED AN AGENT.

Do you need an editor if you self-publish?

Unless you are a skilled professional editor and a copyeditor, yes. You need another set of eyes on your work to find both the sloppy and the dumb. And I say this as someone who has writing a whole lotta fiction and a whole lotta nonfiction. You are going to make mistakes, and you are going to overlook them in your own edits.

Sane doctors don't do surgery on themselves.

Sane lawyers don't represent themselves in court.

And sane writers get a qualified second set of eyes to read what they've done.

Can you recommend an editor or an agent?

No. Again — there are tons of folks out there who present themselves as agents and as editors. And some are legit, and some are crooks. I don't know which are which. My agent is a Commercial Publishing agent, my editors have all been Commercial Publishing editors, and they won't be available for self-publishers — because self-publishing has not equalled the overall quality and consistency (and massive sales numbers) of Commercial Publishing and by doing so proven that it is Real Publishing.

This sucks. It is, as of 2012, still the way things are.

When you buy self-published e-books you love on your Kindle-Nook-iPad-whatever, e-mail the author and ask who he or she used, and whether the writer would recommend this editor again. Right now, word of mouth is all we as self-publishers have.

Can you recommend a book packager?

YES. (Good news at last, hey?)

I use **http://Booknook.biz** for most of my projects, and I have been thrilled with the quality of their work, their work ethic, their commitment to getting the job done right and on time, and their integrity. They are REAL packagers — you pay them for their work, and you own EVERYTHING about your book when they're done.

Are there other great Self-Publishing packagers out there? I'm sure there are. I got lucky on my first shot, though, I have had no reason to look elsewhere.

EXERCISE: Answer the following question in between 100 and 250 words:

Compare WHY you want to write with the processes of self-publishing vs. commercial publishing I've outlined above (ignoring as best you can the smart-ass stuff), and decide which publishing path you want to follow.

---

* *You say there aren't actually all that many writers who've sold more than thirty novels via the Commercial Publishing system?*

You're right. Most writers have their pro careers wiped out by the system itself by the time they finish their third book.

I've survived in the system because I have a streak of persistence that borders on lunatic masochism — but at this point, even I have had enough.

** *"Do the Dance of Shame, Numfar," was the original line, which I've parodied. This is a Joss Whedon/ Angel reference. I'm a committed Joss Whedon fan, and I deeply wish TV guys had a way to self-publish, because I want to see the rest of Firefly, and I would pay joyfully and without hesitation for every episode Joss offered.*

The FAQs About How to Write

How do I stay on track?

I usually get this one from folks who start things well but have a problem finishing them — they either have a lot of good ideas but their stories run out of gas partway through, or they look at what they've done before they finish it and decide that they stink, writing stinks, and life is starting to smell like roadkill too.

This is tough. When I was getting started, I was the author of uncounted thirty-page novels that never made it to page thirty-one. Big plans, no follow-through. I'm not sure what finally got me through those times, but I do remember how I finished my first book, and I think I know why I stalled constantly before that.

I decided when I was around twenty-five that I wanted to finish an entire novel before my next birthday. I sat down and tried to figure out how I was going to do this — I rarely even reached the end of short stories at this point in my career, and the idea of doing two hundred and fifty pages in one project loomed before me like an unclimbable mountain. I figured the number of words I needed (fifty thousand for the genre series book I intended to write). I figured out the number of words I managed to fit on a correctly formatted page. (Roughly 200 in those days.) And I figured out the number of pages I could do in a day when things were going well.

Then I gave myself a page limit, sketched out a tiny little outline, and came up with what I thought would be a pretty nifty last line.

I cannot overstress the importance of this to the beginning writer who's struggling to finish things. It seems totally unrelated, doesn't it? You ask how to keep on track and I say 'set a page limit for yourself and do a little outline.' But it only *seems* unrelated.

Your mind is a complex and tricky thing. It looks at the endless plain of a story stretching before you — a plain that you must traverse with no landmarks, no signs, no map and no compass — and it says, "Nope. Not me. Not today. Not gonna do it, don't think that's my sort of thing, I believe I'll stay here by the river where the water's calm and I know the terrain, thank you. Try me again tomorrow, won't you?" And when you try again tomorrow with a new idea, you again present your mind with an enormous, uncharted terrain.

Even the sketchiest of outlines creates a few landmarks for you and a bit of a map to help you navigate. And when you know how long you'd like the book to run and you set a page limit for yourself, you give yourself a compass. It doesn't tell you which way north is, but it does tell you when you're done for the day, and it lets your mind begin planning the terrain you'll cross tomorrow.

As for all those ideas you come up with while you're working — keep a notebook on hand for them if you'd like. I'll tell you a secret, though. *I don't usually write down the neat ideas that flit through my mind while I'm writing.* The really good ideas will brand themselves on your brain and still be there when you're ready for the next book. The mediocre ones that only seem really good will fall through the cracks and trouble you no more. I don't sweat the ideas I've forgotten. If they were worth my time, I would have remembered them.

And as for thinking that your writing stinks...don't worry about it. Just keep writing. You'll get better and your internal editor will eventually shut up. And then you'll discover that you're a lot better than you thought you were.

What is a chapter and how do you know when you've finished one?

The big secret about chapters is that they're not much of anything but a convenience for the writer, and secondarily for the reader.

There are days when you simply aren't getting the pages done that you want and you desperately want to say you've finished a chapter because your brain needs to focus on something fresh. So you come to the end of a sentence, make the next one a cliffhanger, and break.

Chapter Two appears and you can tell your significant other that you did an entire chapter in one day. You feel better, the book doesn't suffer, and the next day you get to work on a new character or a different location or whatever.

Technically, a chapter needs two things. It should consist of one or more complete scenes, and something ought to change. (Lawrence Block did some chapters that were only one sentence long, and that constituted the entire chapter. The one that comes to mind is "Chip, I'm pregnant," from one of his Chip Harrison books.)

Beyond that whatever you decide constitutes a chapter (and your editor will let you get away with) pretty much does.

I was anal about chapters for a while, insisting that each needed to consist of three scenes of ten pages apiece. This was totally unnecessary from an artistic standpoint, but the Procrustean bed I made for myself while I was doing that taught me some important things.

First, a writer can fit just about any amount of information into just about any amount of space.

Second, that writer will develop a real feel after a while for the pace of the writing — if you must accomplish a certain amount of action in ten pages, then you will, and sooner or later you'll almost know your length to the exact word count.

Third, anyone that anal needs to be smacked upside the head a few times.

I got over that stage eventually. (And you're wondering why I ever got into it in the first place? I was writing ten pages a day and wanted to finish my scene each day and a chapter every three days in order to meet a couple of deadlines. Obvious, huh?)

How long does a book have to be?

Long enough to fit between the covers.

Seriously, though, if we're talking novels for adult readers that are not series books for a specific line (like Harlequin Romances), if you write something that runs from 80,000 to 120,000 words you'll be in the prime marketability range.

Shorter than that and the book will look thin on the shelf and have a harder time convincing readers to part with six or seven bucks. This is a thing called 'perceived value' and you will ignore it at your own risk.

Longer than that and your publisher will have to invest more in paper and printing for each book, and if it's your first novel and he isn't sure it's going to be a blockbuster, he'll have to worry about getting his money out of it.

For series books, write off and request the guidelines. For children's and young adult books, the lengths vary by age, and since I haven't done any of these, I'm not a good source for information. There are books that can tell you what you need to know.

If you're self-publishing, your are the God of your book, and it can be as long as you say. Just remember that *perceived value* is in the eyes of your readers, and you have to deliver a story big enough and deep enough to fulfill reader expectations regarding the money you're charging.

How do I know when my book is good enough to sell?

This is such a reasonable question, and I wish there were a reasonable answer for it. There isn't. You know when an editor calls your house and offers you money for it. Short of that, there isn't any way to tell. If you believe in your book, keep sending it around (while you work on the next one). The fact that it's gathering rejection slips doesn't mean it isn't any good. The Postman Always Rings Twice got its title from the fact that the way the postman let the author know his manuscript had come home in its little brown body-bag again was by ringing the doorbell twice. That book not only sold (eventually) but made its author's reputation and made everyone involved with it a lot of money.

Again, this is the commercial publishing answer. Go back to the Self-Pub FAQs for how you know when you're good enough if you're self-publishing.

What about the schism between art and commercialism? Do I write for the art, or for the money?

What schism?

Okay. You have to remember who it is you're talking to here. I am one of very, very few writers who makes a full-time living from my writing and who doesn't do anything else on the side. So there are people who are going to insist that this fact alone puts me in the camp of the commercial hacks. I think that attitude is stupid, but it is pervasive, and if you want to make money for your writing, you'd better come to grips with the fact that if you do, there are plenty of people out there who will be more than happy to call you a whore.

What you need to remember is that the fact that they believe it doesn't make it true.

People write for one of three audiences. They write for their buyers (publisher, editor, agent, readers), they write for the critics, or they write for themselves.

You can do good work and write for any of these audiences, but you're just as much in danger of whoring your soul if you try to please academe as you are if you try to please your fans.

If you write to please yourself — if you're sitting at your computer telling yourself stories every day that make you laugh, make you cry, make you think — then you're going to do the work that's truest to you.

And that may not become critically acclaimed art, or it may not become commercially successful art, but it will by God be art, and it will be yours, and you will sleep better at night for doing it.

Is it better to start with short stories and work up to novels, or is it better to start with novels?

Depends on what you like and what your goals are. If you dream of being a novelist, start with novels and stick with them. If you want to be the next O'Henry, start with short stories. If you love both, do both.

From the standpoint of sales, I've found that it's easier to sell novels than short stories — there are more markets and they pay a whole lot better. But there are plenty of writers who don't think at novel length, and who would be hurting their work if they spent all their time trying to write novels when they have the sort of mind that bursts with fresh ideas, new characters, and strange twists every day.

And again, here the rules are different for self-publishers. Since you can in fact put out a collection of your short fiction any time you please, you can start out by writing short fiction, and graduate to novels if you're so inclined.

And a note on this — writing a short story and writing a novel are two ENTIRELY different animals. You don't learn how to do one by doing the other.

But if you're already doing both, start wherever you want.

How do you write the synopsis that you're supposed to include with the chapters you send to an agent or editor?

A synopsis is a typed single-spaced single page (two at *absolute* most) that tells the bare bones of your story in present-tense.

Example:

> *David Wagner has a problem. He comes home to find his house broken into, his wife and children gone, and three dead black mice dangling from their tails on his front door. No note, no signs of violence, nothing else but his family taken. The police cannot find any fingerprints in the house — any fingerprints, not even David's or his wife's or children's. There's no sign of forced entry.*
>
> *He is, of course, their primary suspect, and he discovers that he's being framed when....*

Anyway — like that. I was starting to get interested in the idea, and I have to get back to my book. I don't need David Wagner running around in my head looking for his wife and little Tyler and Griffin and the killer of the three black mice. Go all the way to the end of your story, **and write the ending.** Don't be coy and leave a cliffhanger, just tell the editor what happens. Leave out dialogue, description, and minor secondary characters.

I'll tell you now, good synopses are hard to write. Plan to spend a week or two getting it down and refining it and clearing out the deadwood. Focus on the action, and on the main characters and the main storyline. And remember that one page is better that two where a synopsis is concerned.

FAQs About Money

How much should I pay to get my book published?

Commercial Publishing Answer:

Nothing. Not a dime, not half the expenses, not "a modest sum," not anything. Not ever. You don't pay to have your book published. The reason you don't pay to have your book published is as follows: If you're a writer, then writing is your job. People get paid to do their jobs — nurses get paid to nurse, ditchdiggers get paid to dig ditches, and writers get paid to write.

Writers get paid to write.

Writers get paid to write.

Repeat this until it sticks.

Real publishers pay writers an advance. It may not be much of an advance, or it may be more money than you would know what to do with (though I'm sure you would think of something) but they pay. They pay because they believe in your book, and they believe they can sell it and make a profit from it, and they are willing to invest in a product they believe in. They will also pay royalties against the advance, and they will pay extra for subsidiary rights, or else you will hang on to those rights to resell later.

The publishers who are actively soliciting for your manuscript in the backs of magazines, and who pretend to evaluate your manuscript when you send it to them, and who cheerfully write back to you that they are thrilled to accept your wonderful manuscript, and that you will have 10,000 lovely books printed with beautiful covers, professional design, and all you have to do is send them $4000 so that they can start you on the road to being an author, are NOT REAL PUBLISHERS.

They are not starting you on the road to being an author. They will publish anything, because the only thing they believe in is your money. They are lightening your pocket of $4000 to print books that you will not be able to get distributed by bookstores, advertised by marketing departments, or sold. If you deal with such a publisher, you are buying 10,000 (or however many) books that you can use to insulate your basement or give away to friends who will politely accept them and then not read them. And I hope you have a lot of friends. If you pay to have your book published, you aren't really published.

There are two exceptions to the Never Pay To Have Your Book Published rule. The first is if you are well-entrenched in the lecture circuit and you need to have a non-fiction, topic-related book to sell along with your lectures. In this case, go ahead and pay a subsidy publisher to make your book for you. Market it yourself, keep track of your income from it, promote yourself and your lectures mercilessly, and if you do well enough, you may be able to get a real publisher to publish it and distribute it nationwide.

The second time you might want to consider vanity presses is if you want to put together a nice little book that you can give away to your family and friends, and you have the money to spend, and you are under no delusions that what you are doing is in any way related to being published, and you realize that vanity publication is, in the world of publishing, worse than having no publication history at all. If you really want to have a book with your name on it, and you have no interest in making money from writing, go ahead and pay someone to print your book. This is a legitimate route to consider if you're big in genealogy, for example, and you have your entire family tree mapped and you've written a family history. By all means have copies printed and give them to your relatives — this isn't the sort of book a publisher would ever print (unless you have some fascinating, famous relatives).

But otherwise, repeat after me: Writer Beware.

http://www.sfwa.org/for-authors/writer-beware

BOOKMARK this page. Check it regularly. It will save you from horrendous frauds, the loss of your copyright, the loss of your money, and heartbreaks that have been created by scam artists to take advantage of hopeful but naïve writers.

Self-Publishing Answer:

Keep your costs down until you start getting an idea of how much income you'll be bringing in from your books. In the beginning, it will not be a lot. If you're awful, it will never be a lot. If you learn your craft, focus on good storytelling, and write the stories you will want to read, you'll gain a readership over time, and can afford to start spending more per book.

Initially you'll do whatever you can yourself. Priorities that will help you get and KEEP readers, however, are as follows:

- **Quality cover art** (#1 Priority)

- **Professional editing** (OTHER #1 Priority)

- Professional formatting

- Distribution

- Promotion

Do your own promotion. When you're getting started, the person who knows your work best is you, and all the many folks out there who offer to promote for you (for a substantial fee) will give you far weaker results than you'll get on your own.

Do your own distribution (uploading books to the sites from which you'll be selling, like Amazon, Barnes & Noble, Apple iBooks, and so on).

If you're seriously tight for bucks, do your own formatting. I used Scrivener for this book because my budget for it was ZERO dollars. Ditto the editing and the cover art. At the point where your time is more valuable than the price of formatting your own book (and where you know you'll make back the cost in only a month or two, spend the bucks to have your work professionally formatted. Time is more important than money, because if you have the time, you can use it to write, which will eventually make you more money than formatting will save you.

If you have any budget at all, split your budget between professional editing and quality cover art. Keep the split at 50%-50% all the way to the point where you can't afford either someone to edit or someone to do your cover art, and as much as I hate to say this, if you have to do one of those yourself, do the editing. If you have crappy cover art, no one will buy the book to discover you also have crappy editing.

THEN find your nearest and dearest friend who is a big reader, a great speller, and nit-picky as hell, and offer him or her the best bribe you can to read your book and go over it looking for mistakes.

And the INSTANT you can afford it, hire a copyeditor, and release a corrected edition of your book. Don't do a print version of your book until you've had a qualified pair of eyes go over it in detail and you've made all necessary changes, because while you can upload a corrected edition of your ebooks to the different sites and your current readers will get the new version for free, the person who shelled out for your crappy print edition is stuck with all your mistakes.

How do you decide on a reasonable budget?

How much of your savings can you do without for the number of months it will take your book to earn back what you spent on it.

FORMULA:

X amount of money over Y months = BUDGET

For your first several books, until you build up a readership and a backlist, assume that your earnings will be pathetically small. If you have no savings, don't go into your live-on money thinking you'll make it all back. Do the work yourself as best you can.

A $300 investment of $150 for cover art and $150 for a reader that you need to have your FIRST book earn back in three months requires that your book NET $100 a month. Unless you're a screaming whiz at promotion straight out of the gate, you aren't going to get that.

And yes, I know there are self-pubbed writers pulling in $50,000 a month from their work, but if you study their websites, you realize they have hundreds of available books, short stories, and other goodies out there. They have *backlist*.

Until you have BACKLIST, you aren't going to be making a steady income from this.

How much backlist? Six books minimum if you're a genius at promotion. Ten books comfortably, if you're promoting them decently and you have at least some readers who buy one, then buy the rest.

If you have money and understand you're going to be in for a long return on it, spend it to improve your sales and shorten your curve to success. If you don't, work on a do-it-yourself shoestring until your money is working for you.

Finally, to the best of my knowledge, there's no organization out there looking out for self-publishers. So learn to look out for yourself. Get to know other self-publishers. Trade information on artists, copyeditors, book formatters/compilers, and other people you hire to help you out. Keep track of who's good, who's slow, who's dishonest, who to avoid.

How much should I charge for my book?

Commercial Publishing Answer:

I love this question. It is the flip side of "how much should I pay to have my book published?" The droll answer is "you should be so lucky…"

Again, this is not the way the business works. You want to have an agent represent you in the negotiation of how much you're going to get for your book (and how many rights you'll keep and how many you'll sell), but how much the publisher pays for the book is, in the end, entirely up to the publisher. Don't expect a fortune. Don't expect, in fact, to make more than you would have made from flipping burgers part-time for the same number of hours of work for your first novel. $250,000 first-novel advances like the one my first agent, Russ Galen, got for Terry Goodkind are rare indeed. Much more typical is the $5000 I got for my first book, back before I had an agent.

Self-Publishing Answer:

There are ebooks available on Kindle, Nook, the iPad, and other readers that will teach you how to price your self-published work. (Many of these books are also available in print, but cost more.) They're worth the money, and I recommend you search them out and read them.

How much money do writers make?

Mostly not as much as we'd like, though I doubt if either Grisham or King has any complaints. The majority of writers don't make any money at all, or so little that they can't count on it for anything more than taking the kids out for a treat now and then. Most writers don't make a living from their writing, ever.

Looked at in the greater scheme of things, though, most ice skaters never skate in the Olympics, most football players never play in the Superbowl, and most violinists never fiddle in Carnegie Hall. I like your odds of making it as a pro writer a lot better than your odds of making it as a pro football player. You have much more control of your outcome, and you won't age out just as you're starting to get good. And knees are never an issue for a writer.

For those writers who do go pro, money ranges from "starving in a trailer park" to "opulent beyond your wildest dreams of avarice." Assume that there are more "starving in a trailer park" writers than "rolling in the salad" writers and you'll be right. Assume that if you go for this, you'll be one of the former for at least a while. The cool thing about writing is that you always have a chance to become one of the latter.

How much money do *you* make?

My mother always told me it wasn't polite to ask about people's sex lives or how much money they make — and all I can say is that my mail is proof that a lot of people out there weren't raised by my mother.

The answer I'll give: I'm not a "starving in a trailer park" writer anymore (though I did spend my share of time there), but Grisham doesn't need to give me the name of his tax attorney yet.

How do writers get paid?

Commercial Publishing answer:

Infrequently, irregularly, and usually late.

Okay, that's not really as specific as you wanted, was it?

Writers get paid advances, royalties, and "other". I'll discuss advances first. The writer will get a portion of his advance when he signs his contract. He sometimes gets paid another part of the advance when he finishes the first half of the book, paid more of the advance when he turns in the completed manuscript, and sometimes more again when the book is published. A good agent works out the details of how advances come to the writer. There are details like front-ending, back-ending, and the avoidance of basket accounting, etc., that all come within the purview of the advance, and which are best dealt with by you and your agent discussing your needs and your agent going to bat for you to try to see that they get met.

Royalties are in the hands of the publisher, and if you ever see them (and don't assume that you will — most novels never earn out their advance), you will wait a long time before you do. The usual scheme for the payment of royalties goes like this. The publisher agrees to pay royalties in the first accounting period that comes after the end of the first full year after the book's publication. So if your book is published in January 1998 and your publisher's accounting periods are June and December, you might be able to hope for a royalty statement in June of 1999. Maybe.

Don't spend the money yet, though. Royalties are figured "against the advance," meaning that your book has to have earned the publisher enough money that he has already made back your advance from sales before your royalty clock starts ticking. Now, if you got paid a $5000 advance on your first book, the publisher doesn't figure out that he has made back your advance when he sells $5000 worth of books, or even when he has made a net profit (as opposed to gross sales) of $5000. He figures that advance when he has sold enough books that he's made back your advance **out of your royalty percentage**.

Assuming you had a mass market paperback release of your novel and got a relatively standard first novelist's 6% royalty agreement in your contract (this is not good — it's just common), here's what you're looking at. The publisher has to sell a minimum of $83,333 worth of your book before you'll see a dime of royalty money. If your first novel costs $6, he has to sell 13,888 books, right? That doesn't seem so bad.

But it's not even that easy. Your publisher will probably do a print run of around 30,000 books for a first novel. That's about average for a mass market original (a paperback that has never been printed in hardcover or trade paper). If the publisher's reps pitch your title pretty well, he may ship most of those copies to bookstores. Some of them he may give away for free to reviewers and others who might want to sell the book, but the number of gimmes is never very high. Assume you have a first shipping of 26,000 copies. (This is a bit optimistic, but not extreme). If publishing were a kinder and gentler industry, you would have to sell slightly more than half of all the books that shipped at full price (no remainders — you don't get paid for those)...and you would have to do it before bookstores start ripping the front cover off the remainder of their copies and returning them. In a lot of cases, you have about a month. But it isn't a kinder and gentler business. You have something even tougher to contend with, and here's where things get grim.

Publishers have a "reserve against returns" clause that allows them to not count a percentage of your sales because they will use those sales as a buffer against the inevitable returns. Bookstores order titles with a right to return unsold merchandise, but the only part of mass market originals that they return is the front cover. The rest of the book is destroyed. Returns cut seriously into a publisher's profit — he still paid for those books to be printed and shipped after all. Some of your books will be returned; this is a fact of publishing. The publisher knows it, and you had better know it, too. His reserve against returns in your royalty statement can run from a low of ten percent to a high of fifty or sixty percent. This means that you have to sell up to twice as many books in order to start earning royalties. And returns for most first novels are higher than fifty percent. In most cases, much higher.

So if more than fifty percent of your books are destroyed before anyone has a chance to buy them, and if you don't see any royalties until you've sold anywhere from sixty to one hundred percent of your first shipping, how are you ever going to make any money?

You aren't. This is why most writers have a day job. In order to make money, you have to have a high sell-through (the percentage of books your publisher ships minus the percentage of books the bookstores return) and you have to have fairly good-sized print runs. Your publisher has to be willing to keep you in stock — to gamble on the fact that bookstores will keep ordering your older work, and that people will keep buying it. You have to sell the copies of your book quickly, you have to stake out shelf space in chains that prefer to return (destroy) older titles to make space for newer ones, you have to build a reader following, and you have to add new titles to your list on a regular basis in order to give the stores a reason to keep up your backlist (the older books you've written).

Authors whose first three or so books have returns of fifty percent or more are out of the game. Publishers will stop buying from them — not just your current publisher, but also the other publishers you might hope to sell to. Because if you have a publishing history, the first thing any prospective publisher will want to see is your numbers — your print runs, your returns, your total sales, and especially your sell-through. If your sell-through with your old publisher was less than fifty percent, a new publisher will turn you down. Maybe not your book, if he really loves it, but you. This is where pen names can be useful — more than one author with bad numbers has started over with a new name, in essence becoming a first novelist again and acquiring a clean publishing history in the process. It's a bit like being able to become a virgin all over again — but still getting to keep your experience. Which is another reason why writing is a better career choice than pro sports.

So how much of the publication process do you control? You control the quality of the books you write and how frequently you write them. All else is is the hands of an industry where the odds are stacked heavily against you.

This is why most writers are a little crazy. If God owes you any favors, the time to call them in is when you start publishing.

And finally, a discussion of "other" money. From time to time, your agent will send you checks you didn't know were coming. These occur because he's been quietly selling subsidiary rights to your backlist books while you were plugging away at the new project at home. These include foreign rights, book club rights, movie rights, book-on-tape rights, and who knows what else. If you managed to hang on to most of your rights, and if your agent has been talented and fortunate enough to sell them, you'll occasionally open the mailbox to discover a nice surprise. Sometimes a very nice surprise.

This is one of the things that keeps us crazy writers from doing the otherwise drastic and sometimes irrevocable. And no, I'm not talking about suicide. I'm talking about going out and finding the sort of job your mother wishes you had. You can't count on this money. You can't even really hope for it. But when it falls on your head, it sure is nice to get.

Self-Publishing answer:

Self-pubbed writers get paid monthly. Monthly, baby. Do the dance of joy.

MONTHLY.

And if you have a US bank account, the big guys (Amazon.com, Apple, and Barnes & Noble) drop the money straight into your bank account every month, and keep *lovely* records you or your accountant can use at tax time.

Monthly.

And if you have your own little site bookstore, and you sell from there, too, you can also get paid daily.

DAILY.

Yes. *This is the sweetest reason to self-publish.* **You** make the money. **You** keep the money. And you pay the bills and eat regularly.

How do you run a household while writing full-time?

[The writer sits with her eyes closed for just a moment, pondering.]

If you've read the rest of the money questions, you know how hairy the money situation for writers can be. Usually is. Almost always is. [The writer winces and wishes you hadn't asked].

If you're going to write, the safest way to run a household would be to either have a full-time job of your own or to be sharing income responsibilities with someone who is A) very understanding and B) employed in a safe, regular-hours, high-paying job that covers all of your expenses and at least some of your desires.

But most of us who write don't want to keep our day job. We dream of writing as a way out — a way out of low-paying, dangerous or depressing jobs that are all we can get, or out of work that takes us away from our homes or families, or out of the soul-tearing frazzle of hectic, frantic, high-pressure employment. Or perhaps we have physical handicaps that prevent other forms of work. It may be a way out of poverty. A way out of rote. A way out of feeling insignificant.

For me, back a few years when I was recently divorced with two small children, with no child support or alimony, and with a job as a registered nurse, writing was the way I was going to be able to get out of my income-limited and dangerous nursing job (you make enough money as a staff RN that you can survive on your own and feed your children, but you know that the life you're living isn't going to ever be much better than it is at the moment when you're looking at your options), to be home for my kids all the time, and to still have a chance to radically change my standard of living for the better.

I do write full-time and have been doing so since 1992, and my household has no other source of income. This is how I did it.

- I wrote every day.

- I sent stuff out as often as I could.

- I spent less than I made.

- I never used credit (credit cards are the path to destruction for a writer — something I discovered once I'd "made it" but after hard times returned).

- I reused, used up, and made do.

- I banished television from the house, so that the time I had with the kids I actually spent with them.

- I never gave up on my dream.

- I never quit.

If your eyes paused on the little phrase above — "after hard times returned" — you have good instincts. If they didn't, you aren't paranoid enough yet.

A writer is only as secure as his last book's sales, and the publishing industry has a short memory. You can never breathe easy until you have enough money in secure long-term investments that you're living off the interest. I'm not close. Frankly, I'm not even in the "breathing-easy" ballgame yet. If at any point in the game I have three consecutive books that tank, I'm going to be in the line of writers who have to change their names in order to sell, just like the beginner who has the same thing happen. I have the advantages of having had some success, and having a good agent — so with a different name I will probably be able to sell new work. But there are no guarantees. Not ever. No matter how good I am, or how prolific, or how dedicated. Making a living from writing is living on the edge of somebody else's calculator, and the numbers on that calculator are hard and cold and they know no mercy.

[UPDATE: That was true when I wrote it, and kept getting truer the longer I stayed in the game. Which is why I changed games and went indie.}

If you're smart (I wasn't for a while, but a couple of very rough years gave me back my brains) you'll never break the rules I listed above. If you do break them, you'll probably live to regret it.

And now you're thinking, "Why would any human being **do** this?"

Since I quit my day job, I've been broke quite a few times; I've been flush quite a few times. But no matter how rough things got, my kids had food every day and a roof over their heads, and writing has given me relationships with them that I couldn't have had any other way. Writing has given me friendships and challenges that I never could have imagined. It has opened doors, let me reach out to people, let me touch lives. I have seen places I would never have gone to otherwise. I have done things I would never have had the courage to try otherwise.

My life is an adventure, and almost every morning I wake up amazed that I'm the lucky shmuck who gets to do this for a living. Yep — even when I'm broke. Writing is hairy and scary and uncertain, but it's also wonderful and thrilling and a hell of a lot of fun. If I could be anyone in the world doing anything in the world, I wouldn't be Stephen King or Dean Koontz or John Grisham with all their success and all their money...I'd be me, and I'd be doing this. Right here, right now, making it on my own and climbing the mountain by myself.

[UPDATE: All still true. Just a lot less stressful.]

What else could anyone ask for?

Well, the self-publishing answer to that question is....

A writer could ask for self-publishing, where you have control over both your output and your income, and you can keep your backlist in print so your income will get BETTER over time, not worse.

Self-publishing my non-fiction over the past six or so years has given me a stable life. Not a rich one, but a stable one. I can pay bills on time. I don't have nightmares about where the money for the water bill will come from.

I now highly recommend self-publishing as the better answer to commercial publishing.

FAQs About the Business of Writing

How do I keep my work fresh and my enthusiasm up?

Sooner or later, everyone wonders this about any job, and writing is no different, as evidenced by the number of times this question comes in. You want to think you're going to stay as fresh on the fiftieth book as you are on the first, but reading through the works of some of your favorite authors who have been in the business for twenty or more years, you start noticing a tiredness of plot and characterization, a sort of gray sameness that creeps in and leeches the fun out of the latest things they've done. Then there are those other writers who seem to be able to bring everything in them to every single book — they just keep getting better.

I want to be in that second class of writers, and I'm guessing you do too.

Here are the steps I'm taking to improve my odds. I share them with you in the hopes that you'll find them useful. If you have anything additional to suggest, I welcome your comments.

- **Read widely outside of your field.**

No matter how tempting it is to say, "Well, I love romances and I only intend to write romances, so why waste time reading westerns or hardboiled detective novels?" you have to resist. This is, I believe, the single most important tool in the professional's arsenal. Read everything. Read fiction and nonfiction, read old stuff and new stuff, read mainstream and genre, read biographies and how-to's and the labels on the foods you buy.

Don't only read things you like, either. If you hate romances, ask someone who is both knowlegeable about the field and a bit discriminating what some of the good ones are. Pick up two or three and read them from start to finish. Ditto if you hate SF or fantasy or mystery or mainstream or whatever. You can find tools everywhere, and you will find more of them in fields that have been fallow for you for most or all of your life than in the fields that you have been plowing and depleting for years.

If you want to stay fresh, you cannot afford to be a snob. Snobbery is one of the characteristics of a rigid mind...and rigid minds are not full of freshness and vitality.

- ## Write outside of your field.

I'm currently working on a novel that no one might ever see. I've been dinking with it for a few years, doing a couple of pages in my spare time or when I'm stuck on the books that I have contracts for and know I'll get paid for. It's not SF, it's not fantasy, and my agent has already let me know that although he loves the idea and the bits of it he's seen, it's going to be tough to move. I might not be able to sell it, and if I do sell it, I might make first novelist's pay for it.

Doesn't matter. I'm not writing it for the money. Like this page, I'm writing it for love. I love the story, I love the characters, I love the themes and the directions it's taking. And knowing that it's there and that I can work on it whenever I want makes me happy. It reminds me that I am not confined to the walls of the genre in which I work — that I can write anything, that I have no limits except those that I impose on myself. (It sold. Title: *Midnight Rain*.)

My website is something else I do for love. Writing it brings me a lot of happiness, and so do the letters I get from readers telling me that something I've said has helped them. And this page helps me to focus on how I write, and helps me to remember why. Both of those things have kept me going through some rough spots.

- ## Work in other mediums.

I paint; I draw; I write music and play the guitar (though not well); I knit sweaters and crochet lace and afghans; I do beadwork. At times in the past I have spent some time learning the basics of how to play the hammer dulcimer, the cello, and the penny-whistle. I write a middling amount of poetry. None of these things is ever going to earn me a dime (well, maybe the painting might someday, and I have done the maps and such in some of my books, but in general none of this is going to earn me a dime.)

It does allow me to express myself in forms that move beyond the structure of words on page and the linear logic of story, and I suspect it allows my mind to approach my work from angles that it wouldn't otherwise get. I've used my experiences with music and art and crafts in my work, too, but the verisimilitude I've been able to bring to the books because of that has been secondary to the gains I get from having other outlets for creating.

You don't have to be good at any of this stuff to do it. You're doing it for yourself. Cut yourself some slack — you can be a lousy painter and still enjoy the delightful smell of linseed oil and the sensual feel of dabbing paint on canvas, or the homely pleasure of restringing and tuning your guitar and playing a few chords that suddenly sound pretty nice together.

- ## Grab opportunities to learn new things.

Once a week, go someplace in your town that you've never been. Go to a church or synagogue that you don't belong to, in a religion other than yours. Stop by that little one-man museum curated by the old guy at the end of the street. Pick up a book on growing roses just because you've always thought it would be cool to try, and learn all about organic fertilizers and the uses of ladybugs and praying mantises. Take a class in stained glass work or CPR or bookkeeping. Learn to ice skate or tango. Ask the beautician and your accountant and the old woman sitting next to you at the bus stop to tell you about their work.

Sooner or later, these excursions will work their way into your subconscious, and from there begin to filter into your work.

- **Listen more than you speak.**

You only discover the cool things in the universe when your mouth is closed and your senses are open.

- **Pay attention all the time.**

Ask yourself why your neighbor leaves his house at 4:30 every morning and returns exactly one hour later, wearing different clothes. Why does that woman in front of you in the checkout line keep looking over her shoulder? What are those teenaged girls huddled around over there in the corner of the park, and why are they laughing like that? Notice people, cars, buildings, street names, the way light falls on water and on old brick, the smell of the earth by your back door on a hot day in August.

- **Don't write more of the same.**

If you write series books, permit your characters to grow and change. Or write books away from your series. If you write stand-alones, write male and female characters, young and old people, those who have had easy lives and those who have had it rough. If you keep writing the same character and just giving him different names, or telling the same story but from different places, you're going to get stale fast, and the joy will go out of everything you do.

- **Keep the machine in good working order — stay healthy.**

And you're saying,"Eh? Like...exercise and shit like that?"

Oh, yes. Exercise and shit like that. You won't be lifting those bales and toting that hay, but to work your mind, your brain still needs a good supply of oxygenated blood, and healthy highways to get it there and back to the heart and lungs. Twenty minutes of aerobic exercise four times a week or better, and a diet as low in animal products (none is best) and as high in raw fruits and vegetables as you can manage will strip the cholesterol out of your arteries and keep them from hardening. Cadavers from apparently healthy children as young as eight have shown fatty deposits and the beginnings of hardening of the arteries, so no matter who you are or how young you are, this is an issue.

How do I face the computer each day?

It should be fun most of the time. If you're following the steps I've listed above and you're still dreading sitting down in front of the keyboard, and you're still miserable while you're there, you need to reconsider what you want to do with your life. Don't try to make a career from something you hate.

When should I start marketing my book?

If it's fiction, when it's done. If it's nonfiction, when you have a good proposal and some good sample chapters, or when it's done.

How do I treat my writing as a business?

- Write every day.

- Give yourself a page limit and set deadlines for project completion. Write your deadlines in on a desk calendar and meet them.

- Don't answer the phone while you're writing.

- Don't take time off from your writing to do housework or go out to lunch with friends or find the kids' mittens. If this means that you have to write at wierd times of the day, write at wierd times of the day. My work hours are from five a.m. to noon.

- Create a workspace for yourself that is yours alone, even if it's just one corner of a room and your own particle-board mini-workstation.

- Identify yourself as a writer, to yourself and to others.

- Keep all your writing-related receipts.

- Don't accept the judgements of others as having any meaning. If your friends or family suggest that what you're doing is just a hobby and that you shouldn't be wasting your time on it, ignore them.

Do I need an accountant?

If you're spending any money on writing supplies, computers, office equipment or postage, yes. If you're making any money at all, yes. If you're typing with a thirty-year-old Remington on second sheets and only popping for a ream of good paper for your final draft once a year or so, and if you aren't yet selling your work, don't sweat it.

Should I incorporate?

At the point where this crosses your mind, ask your accountant. You'll already be making money, and will have one.

If you aren't making money yet, worry about selling your work first.

What about taxes?

Save all your receipts for everything, follow your accountant's instructions, grit your teeth, and vote.

What about setting up corollary incomes?

It's a good idea. If you want to write for a living and you want to keep writing for a living, even if you never become a wildly famous celebrity author, it's a necessary idea.

The old way of making a living as a writer, when you could write a book a year and live on royalties from your backlist while you wrote future books, is just about dead and gone if you're being published by the mainstream publishers.

This wonderful old model where every book you wrote was an asset that you owned that brought in steady income for you is, however, exactly how self-publishing now works.

Most commercially published books are off the shelves in three months and out of print in their first year. Most writers who get the shot at mainstream publishing are gone after three books. There are exceptions — but those exceptions are big stars, not solid midlisters. If you're building your life on the hope that you're going to be a star, you don't have a viable business plan.

Backlists have become nonexistent unless you regain your rights when your books go out of print. If you own your backlist rights, build your own deep backlist via Amazon.com, Barnes & Nobel, Apple, and other sites that let you republish your work professionally (and protect your work with DRM).

Look at mainstream publishing with some caution — publishing as a whole is going through this bizarre transformation right now, with no one able to guess how it's going to look in five years. Or ten.

Do I follow my own advice? Yes. I have some of my work available through the three outlets mentioned above now, and though it's time-consuming, I'm prepping more all the time. When I get my backlist published, I'm going to publish my new novels directly, starting with *Warpaint*, the second Cadence Drake novel. I've created writing courses in various shapes and sizes. If you don't know how the publishing scene is going to shake out…and NOBODY right now knows that… you need to build a broad base with your work so that even if parts you were counting on to work don't, you still have money coming in from other parts while you can figure out what to do next.

My Three Most Frequently Asked Questions

Can you read something I wrote?

No. The short answer is that I don't have the time and even if I did, my agent forbids it.

The long answer is that, first, society being what it is today, on my agent's advice I don't look at anything that hasn't already been sold to a publishing house. I have ideas for the next hundred years and have no interest in stealing anyone else's, but if I don't read anything that hasn't already been sold to a publisher, I'll never find myself in a situation where I have to prove that fact in court.

Second, this page has already generated thousands of letters. Roughly 25% of the people who write to me ask me if I'll read their novel, their short story, their poetry, or their background, and tell them how to fix it, and maybe put in a good word with my agent or my publisher for them — and this in spite of the fact that I've noted elsewhere that I don't read manuscripts. If I gave up writing, I could spend every minute of my time doing this, or I could keep writing and give up my family life, but I'm not interested in doing either. I like writing for a living and I love my family.

You don't need to have a writer read your manuscript in order for it to get published. You need to learn to read it with a critical eye, and be willing to change what you see that needs to be fixed. These are essential skills for any professional, and until you've learned them you won't be able to sell. And the only way you can learn them is to work at it. I know this is hard, and hearing it may be disappointing, but there is no easy way to succeed.

Can you hook me up with a publisher or editor or agent?

No. When you've written something publishable, start sending it around. While it's circulating, start work on the next thing. You will eventually find your agent and your editor and your publisher. But again, there's no easy way. You don't need an in — you just need patience and faith and to have written something good.

If I supply the idea, would you collaborate with me on a book?

No. But we can do it the other way if you'd like. Here's an idea. The hero is a guy who wakes up one morning to discover that his wife is gone and there's this little doll lying on her side of the bed. No note, no nothing — just the doll. No sign of a break in, no sign of anything missing except his wife, no sign of violence. He's scared, he can't figure out what has happened...and I'm not sure what happens after that.

You take that idea, and spend nine months or a year or whatever working it into a finished novel, and sell it, and when you're done, credit me with coauthor status because I came up with the idea and send me half of your advance and half of your royalties from now until the end of time. Also half of all subrights sales.

Or better yet, don't. You're welcome to the idea — if you use it and sell it, good for you and have fun with the money. You don't owe me anything. But now I hope you can see why writers aren't thrilled when someone asks them this question.

Holly Lisle

My Five Worst Career Mistakes, and How You Can Avoid Them

I've written some very good books. I debuted well — my first novel, *Fire in the Mist,* won the Compton Crook Award for Best First Novel and I was a finalist twice for the John W. Campbell award for Best New Writer. I've gotten much better with experience. My books are consistently rated highly by *Amazon.com* readers — many of them have five-star ratings. I've had wonderful reviews, I get letters and e-mails regularly that say "I don't read fantasy but I read your stuff," and "I read a lot of fantasy and you're my favorite author," and I've even a really nice note from one of my copyeditors, telling me that she loved working on my book even though she kept getting sucked into the story, because it was a great story.

And yet I've had to struggle to make it in writing. I'm still struggling, nearly ten years into my career. Why?

ADDED NOTE: Twenty years into my career, I'm not still struggling. I'm not rich, but I'm self-sufficient and I don't have to worry about paying my bills on time. Self-publishing changed everything for me.

I made five big, avoidable mistakes when I was just getting started. I didn't have anyone to tell me not to make them, I didn't know any better, and as a result I'm having to seriously consider working under a pseudonym, something I swore when I started that I would never do.

ADDED NOTE: I didn't (except for one work-for-hire book right at the point before I discovered self-publishing). I'm glad I didn't. My readers only have to look for me by one name.

I didn't have anyone to tell me not to make these mistakes, but you have me. It's hard writing about them now — I cannot look at what I've done and think about what I could have done without feelings of deep regret. Please listen. What I have to say here can save your career from sinking before it even starts.

MISTAKE NUMBER ONE — I did not find a publisher who published my genre well.

I submitted *Fire in the Mist* to only one publisher, and I chose that publisher not because of careful consideration of that publisher's list, and not because that publisher had shown a consistent pattern of creating bestsellers in my chosen genre, but because I had already signed a contract to do a collaboration with a published friend at that house, and I saw that as an "in" that would get my solo novel read more quickly. Bad, bad reason to choose a business partner.

The book sold, and I didn't give my decision a second thought. Who can think with an editor on the phone saying, "We want to buy your book?"

So my fantasy novel was accepted in a publishing house that routinely creates bestsellers and best-selling authors in SF, but that has never created a fantasy bestseller or in-house best-selling fantasy author. This was a bad sign, but I didn't know it. The publisher loved SF, but considered fantasy a weak-minded step-sister — he was a nice guy and great to work with, but he put together his fantasy line to fill in a perceived hole in his list, not because he loved fantasy. I didn't know that, either, but if I had been less naïve and less impetuous, I could have figured it out.

So my books didn't matter to my publisher. He had a financial stake in them, but no *personal* stake. Unlike the SF novels that he loved and wanted to see succeed, my books were simply product that he needed to fill out his monthly list. He didn't respect them, he didn't respect what I did, and so he didn't fight for them the way he fought for his SF line.

So how can you avoid making this mistake?

Do your research. Look at the books published in your genre by the various publishers you're considering. Which of these books have sold well? Which are labeled bestsellers, indicating that the publisher can successfully bring a book to the attention of the book-buying public? Which are stocked well by chains, indicating that the publisher can successfully negotiate the hellish computerized chain ordering system? Which are on the shelves with other books by the same author, indicating that the publisher can keep his writers in print and support their backlists?

Only submit your book to those houses that have already proven they'll be able to support it. Don't be an experiment in an expanding list, don't be a shelf-filler at a house that prefers books of other sorts, don't be "the next big star" in a house full of one-book wonders and three-book sinkers.

MISTAKE NUMBER TWO — I wrote collaborations instead of focusing on my own work.

I was sitting at the dinner table at a nice restaurant with my publisher, and he said to me, "Next, I'd really like to see a collaboration from you."

I said, "I did one collaboration, but that was it. It was a lot of work for less money than what I can make on my own, and I don't want to do that again. I want to do another Arhel novel."

He looked hurt. "At this publishing house, we like our writers to be team players. We've found that collaborations help introduce new readers to a writers' work, and we would like to get your name out there."

I didn't want to be labeled "not a team player." I was young and dumb and I trusted that my publisher would want the same thing from my career that I did, and that he wouldn't make suggestions that would actively hurt me.

So learn this now. **Writers are not "team players."** We're individual, independent businessmen and businesswomen and the whole frikkin' point of being a writer is that you own your business, you own your work, you own your life, you own your time, and you do things the way you want to do them. I was a MORON for allowing a hurt look from a clever businessman steer me away from my previous — and much smarter — plan.

I was just flat-out wrong. In almost every instance, a collaboration is a way for a publisher to get a book with a big name author on the cover without paying the big name author's price. The publisher gets some young, dumb, eager writer who wants to be a team player and he offers that writer and the big name author a sum of money that is less than the big name gets, but may be equal to or more than what the newbie gets. The big writer takes half to two thirds of the money, the newbie writes the book. There are variations on this theme, and I've tried most of them, and in only one instance has a collaboration earned out for me. I've done eight. If I'd done twenty, only one would have earned out for me, and that one earned out because the other writer is that rare exception in the field — someone whose name can sell a collaboration.

If I had it to do over again, I wouldn't touch collaborations. Not even the ones I had fun writing, not even the ones that introduced me to some great collaborators, not even the one that still nets me a couple hundred bucks in royalties every six months. The biggest thing collaborations have done for me is hurt my overall sales average, and anything that hurts the salability of your solo work is a bad thing.

What can you do to avoid this mistake?

Easy. Don't do collaborations. Writing isn't a team sport, and you are not a team player. You are a writer, and you're in business to create your own customers. You're opening a store, you're inviting people in to buy, and they are going to be looking for your products. They are not looking for your products diluted with the products of strangers. They want what you have to offer, and if you remember that, you'll keep yourself out of trouble.

MISTAKE NUMBER THREE — I broke a successful series at publisher request.

I had my career mapped out before I sold the first book. I was going to write an open-ended series of stand-alone novels set in the world of Arhel, the magical land in which I set my first novel. I had sketchy outlines for about fifteen books. I would have had a lot of fun doing them.

I sold the first book and it did surprisingly well, winning me an award, getting me nominated for a couple of others, hitting the Locus Bestseller list for two months running (something of a feat for a first novel by a previously unpublished writer with no background in something like short fiction.) And it sold well on the stands, requiring a second printing in relatively short order. I sold the second book in the series, and it was a bit of a sophomore slump, but it was still a strong story. On the strength of the sales of the first book and the completion of the second book on time and in acceptable form, my publisher offered me a three-book contract.

And I said, "Fantastic. What do you want to see?"

And he said, "Anything but another Arhel novel."

And I said, "Oh. Okay, I guess. I have some ideas for other books."

That was the wrong answer. The right answer would have been, "I'm willing to open up new areas in Arhel. I'm willing to introduce new characters in Arhel. But I'm not willing to leave Arhel."

It usually takes at least five books to get a successful series established. I didn't know this. Authors who want to work in a series that they've established need to have five books on the shelves in that series before they start breaking out into unrelated books. They need to establish their reader base. I didn't know this either. You don't break a series that's starting strong after two books in order to write outside your series universe...and I didn't know this, either. I eventually wrote book three of that series, but it had been too long between books one and two, and the third book got lost.

I was young and dumb. Now I'm not. I have a series currently in progress with a new publisher. The series was strong enough that it sold to England and Germany, too. The first two books debuted at #1 on the Locus Bestseller list (a SF/Fantasy genre list.) Both have sold in decent numbers, both have been wonderfully reviewed. The third is finished, and it's the best book of the three. (Not yet in print as I write this, but completed and in the typesetting stage.) So, after three books, my editor wanted to buy another book from me. But she wanted to see something else — because she wanted to "rest" the series. This time I refused. I sold the fourth book in the series, and am writing it now. Will doing more books in this series allow it to find its audience and allow me to establish a solid foothold in the genre? I don't know. But this time I intend to find out.

AND THE ANSWER TO THIS: No. Because there was another process at work when I sold my all my series, and it took me a while to understand how that process applied to me. It's the reason commercial publishing kills most writing careers in three books, the reason most series are dead a week after book two hits the stands — though the writer is unlikely to find this out until after he's finished book three and wants to write more books in the series...and it's the reason you can never find all the books for any series except New York Times bestsellers on the shelves.

I wrote it all out in a long, detailed post on my weblog, and you can read it here:

Ordering to the Net, or How to Kill a Career in Three Easy Books

http://hollylisle.com/selling-to-the-net-or

How do you avoid this mistake?

If you're planning on writing a series, stick to your plan. Don't "rest" your series, don't alternate with non-series books, don't wander around outside of the concept of the series itself. Stick to your world, stick to your characters...and stick to your guns.

If the first and second books tank, you're going to <u>have</u> to write something else. No one is going to buy books in a series that is doing poorly. But if you get rolling well out of the starting gate, keep yourself in the race.

ADDED NOTE: More importantly, if you're planning on writing a series, self-publish it.

It's the ONLY way you can guarantee you'll have the chance to finish it, it's the ONLY way you can guarantee the whole series will remain in print, and if it hits the New York Times Bestseller list, publishers will come begging you to publish it....

...At which point you'll have to decide whether you'd rather make 70% of gross and get paid every month as a self-publisher, or 15% of net with rare six-months-after-your-advance-earns-out royalty statements as a commercially published author.

MISTAKE NUMBER FOUR — I over-committed, accepting too many contracts of the wrong types.

Depending on the hole you dig yourself into, this can be a tough mistake to avoid. I was short on money — I'd quit my day job too early in my career, I was the sole support for my little family, and the offer of additional contracts for collaborative work seemed like a Godsend — extra money for less work than I would have to do on solo novels.

(And you're thinking, But she said collaborations are <u>more</u> work than solo novels. You're right. They are. But I didn't know that at the time.)

At the very worst point in my career, I think I owed my publisher seven books. They were contracted. I'd already been paid my portion of the tiny advance, and had spent the money to live on. I couldn't afford to buy my way out of those contracts. I was writing for poverty money, and I couldn't move to another publishing house that might pay me better because I was obligated to my current publisher, and I couldn't live on what I was making, and no more money would come in until I finished the contracted books.

I wrote my way out of most of my obligations, but it was hard, hard going. I eventually managed to pay back my portion of the advance money for a collaborative trilogy when it became clear that my collaborator had no intention of ever fulfilling his part of the contracts and that if they were to get written, I would have to do them as solo novels — but still get paid for collaborations that would be sold as collaborations and that would sink like collaborations.

At which point, I moved on to another publisher, abandoning a backlist of books I love.

ADDED LATER: The rights for all of MY books from that publisher have reverted to me. The rights for the books where I was senior collaborator have reverted to me as well. The rights for those other collaborations? All gone. DON'T collaborate.

How can you avoid this mistake?

If you owe the book you're writing plus two more, you're in as deep as you need to get. Don't accept another contract or another advance, no matter how much you need the money or how tempting it is. Wait. Finish what you owe. Get a part-time job washing dishes or waiting tables or whatever you have to do to keep your mind clear while bringing in survival money. When you're down to one book owed but unfinished, you can start thinking about selling something else.

ADDED NOTE: Or publish your work yourself.

MISTAKE NUMBER FIVE — I mistook business relationships for friendships, and acted accordingly.

My publisher took me out to dinner. Called me up from time to time to chat about the state of publishing. My editor and I went to a Ren Faire together and had various breakfasts and lunches together, and had a great time discussing my books when I sent them in. We played practical jokes on each other. I had fun.

So I thought my publisher, my editor and I were friends. I made business decisions based on a sense of personal loyalty, trusted that my friends would not suggest courses of action that would be bad for my overall career…and I got burned.

How do you avoid this mistake?

When you sell your book to a professional publisher, you are selling a commodity to a business, and you are a businessman dealing with a corporation, and *you will forget this truth at your own peril.* No matter how friendly everyone is when your work is selling well, remember that you and your books are commodities, subject to market fluctuations, and that when your books' popularity is down, yours will be, too.

Have fun, enjoy the companionship and camaraderie you may develop with the people who buy your books...but remember your bottom line. I guarantee you your publishing associates will. If you do this, you won't get your feelings hurt, you won't make decisions based on a loyalty that does not run both ways, and you will be more aware of what is being done with your work and how it affects you.

ADDED LATER: Or self-publish. It's a viable option now. The better option, if you have the courage to pursue it.

And here's a freebie, for what it's worth.

MISTAKE NUMBER SIX — I quit my day job too soon.

I tell you this because its true, not because I think it will make any difference in your decision-making when your own opportunity to quit the day job comes. I should have been making as much money from royalty income as I was from my day job. I'm still not making that much money from royalties — if I were to follow my own advice, I'd still be working full time and writing on the side.

And, frankly, I would quit too soon again, even under the same circumstances, and even though I know how hard things have been, how hard they are, how hard they may be in the future. If I wouldn't take my own advice on this, why should you?

Well, it's good advice. It's the truth.

But I'd rather be writing and poor than nursing and secure. Because the fact is, in spite of the mistakes I've made, I'm still doing the thing I love. I'm still getting paid for it. I still love getting up and going to work in the morning, sitting at the keyboard and creating new worlds and new people and new magic. If I were just in it for the bucks, I would have been long gone by now.

I'm in it for love. I'm here for the long haul — one way or another, under my own name or under a pseudonym, I'm going to be writing books.

When you get up before your alarm clock goes off most mornings because you're excited about what you're doing, you're doing the right thing with your life. I am. I have no doubts about that.

I hope you don't either.

ADDED LATER: All of this remains true. But not having to worry about bills is SO much better than living in dread (or having the water turned off). Knowing that you can write a book, put it up for sale, and have it start adding money to your bank account right away, even if that money isn't a huge amount on its own, is wonderful. Knowing that your series won't be cancelled, your books won't go out of print, you won't be held captive to someone else's contract — for all of these reasons, I'm sleeping better now than I did during the first sixteen years of my career.

Ten Keys to Designing A Series Character You Can Live With (Forever)

Series sell. They acquire an audience that keeps coming back for more. They make their authors money — the majority of fiction writers who survive on their writing income write series.

But the same strong world and strong concept and strong characters that draw in the readers can start to feel like a trap to the writer. You're stuck with your world. However you made it, that's the way it's going to be. You're stuck with your concept. That's the tie that binds your characters to your world.

But you can do something with your series characters — and it won't be Arthur Conan Doyle's solution: throwing Sherlock Holmes off a cliff. You can't kill them. You need them.

So, from the very first book, make them people you can live with for the long haul.

How? Here are ten keys to creating a series character you can live with. Use some of them or all of them to make sure you have enough room in your series to breathe.

Give your character plenty of room for change and growth.

Start your character when he's young and relatively innocent. He'll accumulate scars even faster than you will — let him have a mostly clean slate on which to accumulate them. You'll find exceptions to this rule on the shelves — series characters who debuted as older men or women. But these old characters — both Miss Marple and Hercule Poirot come to mind — don't age or change. They're set pieces who go about the business of resolving their stories, but they never surprise. If you've read one Miss Marple mystery, you've pretty much read them all. (And I've pretty much read them all, and the Hercule Poirot books, too.) Agatha Christie seemed content enough writing characters who never changed...but I can't think of anyone now who's doing that successfully.

Two writers whose characters started young and grew come immediately to mind, though. The first is Robert B. Parker, who created and still writes the enduring character Spenser. We first met Spenser as a brash young man with some polish as a boxer and a knack for getting himself into ugly situations. He's now pushing the high end of middle age, with the creaking joints and heavy past of someone who has truly lived his life. He's a marvelous character, and I imagine Robert B. Parker still enjoys sitting down and writing Spenser novels...because Spenser can, and frequently does, surprise you.

[UPDATE: Well, he's dead now, and the world is poorer without him. But he wrote until he died, and his books were still wonderful up to and including the last one.

He's my model. I want to do what he did, both as long and as well.]

The second writer who has done something wonderful with a series character is Lawrence Block. Block writes a couple of different series, and his light Bernie Rhodenbarr mysteries are a blast...but his dark Matt Scudder mysteries are brilliant. We first meet Matt Scudder as a heavy-drinking ex-cop who accidentally shot and killed a kid while on duty, and who abandoned his family for a lot of sad reasons. Over the course of many books, we watch Scudder grow up, come to terms with the mistakes he's made in his life, quit drinking, find real love, and become someone you want to know. He's always someone you care about. And he solves a mean mystery, too.

No matter what genre you want to write in (or even if you want to write mainstream), and no matter whether you're male or female, you owe it to yourself and to your writing to read these books. The Spenser novels and the Matt Scudder novels have something to teach you.

Give your character some endearing qualities that make you want to visit with him or her again and again.

Make your character idealistic. Give him a soft spot for kids or dogs. Give her a passion for chocolate, or for rescuing the down-and-out. Create for him or her a sheer joy in living that transcends the mire into which you are eventually going to throw this poor shmuck. You have to like spending time with this person — over the years, you're going to be giving him or her as much of your time as you give to a spouse, and more than you give to a best friend. Make sure you share some common loves.

Give your character serious problems that he or she can't resolve in one book, or even ten.

Spenser deals with the mob and crime in Boston. Neither the mob nor Boston criminals are going anywhere anytime soon. Spenser could live forever and still not run out of enemies to fight. Matt Scudder is dealing with New York's criminals. Same story.

In a fantasy series, you'll have the rival wizards' college, or the nightmare creatures that live just over the border, or the poisoned magic that pours down from the North Pole every winter. In a western series, you'll have the Civil War or the marauding Indians or the encroaching Whites or the ever-present bandits (depending on how historically accurate or politically correct you want to be). In a mainstream series set against the backdrop of World War I, you have World War I.

In each instance, you have built into your universe a problem that is bigger than your hero — bigger than any hundred heroes that you could throw against it, or any thousand.

Racial or territorial rivalries make good base problems, as do religious differences, long-running wars, areas of great poverty butted up against areas of great wealth, class struggles, historical enmity (a la the Montagues and Capulets in *Romeo and Juliet,*) and so on. Make sure your series character has one of these base problems to supply him with a long series of struggles, and you with a long series of books.

Give him or her several real, deep character flaws.

With Matt Scudder, it was the drinking for a long time. With Spenser, it's a blend of bull-headedness and an impetuous streak, combined with delusions of immortality.

Your character can't be perfect or you won't have anywhere to go with him. Readers won't be able to identify him. He can be truly and genuinely good (as Spenser is good) but he can't be a God. He has to be a human, and complex, real humans have complex, real flaws.

Give your character a few friends as interesting as he is, and as deep.

I admit to wanting to kill Susan Silverman, Spenser's long-time girlfriend/ lover/ live-in companion. She is such a shallow bitch. I want to see him find a real woman, and I know he never will, and that's sad. Spenser's other main friend, Hawk, however, always interests me. He's always deeper than he seems, always knows more than you think he does, always surprises. Hawk is a *great* series character.

When you're developing your own series, give as much thought to the people your main character hangs out with and struggles with as you do to him. Don't just give them a hair color, and eye color, and an interesting twitch or two that they exhibit under pressure. Make them real.

Give your character an interesting line of work, something that you won't mind knowing as well as you know your own.

Whatever your character does is going to become your second job — with luck, for a whole lot of years. If you don't give a damn about police work, you'd better not make your main character a cop. If you aren't interested in the military, don't make her a soldier. If you hate horses, avoid both the racetrack and the cavalry.

Give this some real thought. As much thought as you put into becoming a writer.

...Maybe more.

Make sure your character's principle locale interests you.

What goes for work goes twice for locale. You're going to need something fairly big — a whole town that you've developed with tremendous depth will do, but a city is better. A county or small country would be better yet. An entire planet will give you the most latitude, and the most opportunity to avoid boredom. You need to set up any globetrotting tendencies from the start, though.

Give your character a deep, fascinating history.

There's nothing like a checkered past for giving the writer an opportunity to introduce lost loves in distress, illegitimate children in need, old enemies gone but never forgotten, and little skills that come in handy in a pinch. Establish at least the bones of your character's past in your first book, and mine that past faithfully and deeply for real gems in future books.

Give your character at least one really good, long-term enemy — someone who will stay to the background and survive for years. Someone your hero <u>needs</u> somehow.

Ideally, this will be some sort of enemy he's made in the past, one who has the goods on him in some way, or who has something he needs, or who has access to special skills he can't acquire in any other way. This enemy won't be the villain of your individual books, but will be a shadowy presence, threatening from the distance.

Give your character a theme.

Spenser is the slightly battered white knight, rescuing the helpless. Matt Scudder is the fierce and wounded avenger of the unjustly dead. Your character needs to have a reason for going on, a reason for doing what he or she does long after any normal person would throw up hands and say, "Enough, already. I'm getting a job at the Quickie Mart." This reason, this compelling urge forward in the face of insurmountable odds, is your character's theme...and may well be one of your own.

Ten keys. Ten ways of opening a door to more space in a series, more room to work and move around. Ten pointers toward longevity. Here's my key-ring. I hope I'll see you on the shelves. For a long, long time.

How to Make Every Story Better Than the Last

Plenty of writers get to a publishable level of writing, and their books become all the same, and more of the same. "If what I'm writing now is selling, why change anything?" they ask, and it's all too easy to look at their financial success and say, "Yes, why?" They're coasting, spinning their wheels and not going anywhere — yet because their books keep selling, they have no financial impetus to keep pushing themselves or making their work better.

And you're saying, "I should have such a problem."

But if there's no challenge in your work, why bother getting out of bed in the morning? If you've already done the best thing you're ever going to do, what do you have to live for? If you aren't changing...you're dead.

I stop buying books by writers who haven't learned anything new in the last five years. If they haven't gotten anything new out of their lives to put into their books, I might as well re-read the last book they wrote that mattered to them.

I want to read better books. And I want to write better books. And this is the way I challenge myself to make each of my books better than the one before. Maybe you'll find something here that will keep you fresh and help you love your writing long after those who never wanted to change have stagnated, or fossilized.

Take planned risks.

If you've always written in first person, force yourself to write a book in third person. If you've always kept your distance from your characters, force yourself to write one story locked tightly inside your main character's skull, able to use only that character's senses and knowledge. Write something from the point of view of someone completely unlike you — someone you don't understand and don't think you ever could understand. Write a story from the point of view of a dog...and not a cutsie anthropomorphic dog, either, who thinks human thoughts. Write from inside a real dog, who doesn't think in words and who is driven by inhuman desires and guided by inhuman senses. Stretch the boundaries of who you are — stretch the boundaries of what you know and have allowed yourself to experience.

Scare yourself.

If you follow my first suggestion, you are going to hit places where you cannot figure out how to write a scene. It will be too deep, too emotional, or too personal for you to want to tackle it, and you'll be tempted to take the easy way out — to skip that scene or to write around it. Don't give in to temptation. Now is the time to strip yourself naked and walk off the cliff. There's water at the bottom, and you'll discover that flying naked through the air can feel pretty good, and that you're a hell of a lot better swimmer than you could have imagined. But the only way you're going to discover that is if you jump.

Dare to explore the places that scare you. Those are the ones that have your best writing hidden inside of them.

Allow the unexpected to happen.

Characters sometimes grab the bit between their teeth and take off in directions you didn't expect — and if you aren't a horseman, this image doesn't convey much of raw power or raw terror to you, so I'm going to give you a story from my personal experience. I was thirteen. I had a horse — my parents got him for me from one of those kids' camps that keeps horses over the summer and looks for places to board them over the winter. He was mine for a season, and while he was mine, I loved him dearly.

He and I went out riding on a bitterly cold Ohio afternoon, when the sky was a frozen white blue and the glare on the patchy snow shot like lasers into my eyes. He was skittish, my mind was on the way the breath curled from his nostrils and the busy twitching of his ears, and when two pheasants blasted out of a snow bank on the dirt side road we were traveling along, neither of us was prepared. He grabbed the bit in his teeth, preventing me from slowing him down or stopping him by sawing on the reins, and took off at a bucking gallop down the dirt road. He didn't stop until he hit a paved road...and the only reason he stopped then was because his hooves went out from under him and he went down and I jumped off fast enough to save myself from being crushed or breaking a leg. But I landed on my left knee and still have a hell of a scar from it. I was scared to death. We got off the highway with the help of a lady who lived on that corner out in the country and who had apparently seen us. We didn't get run over.

But I found out what it's like to be on the back of a thousand pounds of racing, kicking, panicking animal with no way to steer and no idea of what is going to happen next. It's a shitty feeling.

But it makes a great story.

And you're in this for the story, not for how good you feel while you write it. When your character grabs the bit in his teeth, give him his head. Let him run. Trust him not to get the two of you killed. Maybe you'll end up someplace grand, and if you don't, at least you'll have had one hell of a ride.

Lose track of time.

Take the clocks off your desk, turn off your timer, and let yourself fall into the world you created for as long as you can stay there. Writing with one eye on the clock will give you work about as inspired at that which you did when you were in high school and waiting for the last bell to ring.

Ask yourself the hard questions about life, and allow yourself to be surprised by your answers.

Don't always write stories where you're sure of the moral position of each of the characters. Give your folks some dilemmas that you yourself haven't managed to figure out yet. Let your characters batter out the various positions among themselves. Think your way through each of their positions while you write. You'll learn more about yourself than you expect to, and you may find that you're surprised by what you discover.

Above all...believe.

Believe that what you are doing matters. It does. You can be a creative force in the universe, a destructive force in the universe, or someone cowering behind the curtains, closing his eyes and waiting for life to be over because he's too afraid to move. The fact that you choose creativity is glorious. Believe that you can reach out with your words and change a life. You can — if the life you change is your own, so much the better. Believe that you are doing something to make your part of the world a better place for for yourself, for your family, for the people you care about. You are.

Keep writing. Keep believing. And never give up on your dreams.

Final Thoughts

Writers often present writing as some mystical, magical act of God that only the elite few who have been touched by the Muse at birth dare pursue. It isn't.

These writers, and I can list a stack of them right off the top of my head, will claim that the process of writing is unknowable — that when they sit, they cannot explain what happens, but story magically appears to them, and that this is the way all writing works, and therefore writing is unteachable and only those born knowing how to write will ever do so.

Pardon my French, but *bullshit*.

They don't know how *they* write, and they think the cloud of ignorance surrounding them like fog is necessary for them to create. It *is* entirely possible to write without having the faintest clue about the writing process, or about how your own mind works.

It is, however, impossible to write consistently if you don't understand the writing process, and these writers are the ones who will write books where they miss their endings, meander through plotless hell, and lose characters or kill them because they can't figure out how to get them out of the messes they've gotten them into.

These are the writers who, because they don't know how they do what they do, do worse work the longer they write, repeating what worked before because they have no idea what else to do, but with no new passion or insight to bring to the table.

These are the writers who start a brilliant series, and falter four books down the road because they never had any idea how it was going to end, and they don't understand how to go back and pick up the threads they've dropped from the beginning to weave into a coherent whole.

These are the writers who go chasing down the rabbit hole of booze or drugs, hoping to find what they have mistaken as magic, which is nothing more than the collaboration of their right and left brains, their subconscious and conscious minds — and by chasing inspiration in the bottom of a bottle, killing the collaboration of their mind and their Muse for good. Brains don't work well when pickled or fried.

You will find joy, exuberance, excitement, challenge, frustration, fascination, and even, from time to time, compulsion in writing. What you will not find is mystical magic. Everything in your writing comes from you, and the more you know yourself, your passions, how you think, WHY you think, and how to tease your subconscious mind into working with your conscious mind, the better you'll write. You weren't born to write, and neither were the writers who claim they were.

They *chose* writing.

You *choose* writing.

People aren't "born lawyers," they aren't "born doctors," and they aren't "born writers."

If you want to learn to write, you can. If you're willing to push yourself to learn how to write *well*, you can. There are folks who are better doctors, and better lawyers, just as there are folks who a better writers — but if you want this and are willing to work for it, you can have it. You can make it happen for yourself.

Have courage. Have persistence. Never think that you know enough. I've been doing this seriously since 1994, and I'm still learning new things about writing every day.

The day you think you know it all is the day your work will start to weaken.

Write regularly. Write daringly. Write while embracing your fear, and saying what you mean anyway.

But most of all, write with joy.

Holly Lisle

March 9, 2012

About the Author

Holly Lisle is the author of more than thirty published novels (and counting), including the recent re-release of her award-winning first novel, **Fire in the Mist**, and her upcoming re-release of **Cadence Drake: Hunting The Corrigan's Blood**, which will kick off the ten-book Cadence Drake series.

Holly had an ideal childhood for a writer…which is to say, it was filled with foreign countries and exotic terrains, alien cultures, new languages, the occasional earthquake, flood, or civil war, and one story about a bear, which follows:

"So. Back when I was ten years old, my father and I had finished hunting ducks for our dinner and were walking across the tundra in Alaska toward the spot on the river where we'd tied our boat. We had a couple miles to go by boat to get back to the Moravian Children's Home, where we lived.

"My father was carrying the big bag of decoys and the shotgun; I was carrying the small bag of ducks.

"It was getting dark, we could hear the thud, thud, thud of the generator across the tundra, and suddenly he stopped, pointed down to a pie-pan sized indentation in the tundra that was rapidly filling with water, and said, in a calm and steady voice, "That's a bear footprint. From the size of it, it's a grizzly. The fact that the track is filling with water right now means the bear's still around."

"Which got my attention, but not as much as what he said next.

" 'I don't have the gun with me that will kill a bear,' he told me. 'I just have the one that will make him angry. So if we see the bear, I'm going to shoot him so he'll attack me. I want you to drop what you're carrying, run to the river, follow it to the boat, get the boat back home, and tell everyone what happened.'

"The rest of our walk was very quiet. He was, I'm sure, listening for the bear. I was doing my damnedest to make sure that I remembered where the boat was, how to get to it, how to start the pull-cord engine, and how to drive it back home in the dark down the Kwethluk River's looping, slough-crossed course, because I did not want to let him down.

"We were not eaten by a bear that night…but neither is that walk back from our hunt for supper a part of my life I'll ever forget.

"I keep that story in mind as I write. If what I'm putting on paper isn't at least as memorable as having a grizzly stalking my father and me across the tundra following us and our bag of delicious-smelling ducks, it doesn't make my cut."

You can find her, her novels, her writing courses, 100,000 words of free writing articles and workshops, her weblog, and more at:

http://HollyLisle.com

My Writing Courses

I offer both short, specific courses about specific areas of writing fiction, for example, plot, character creation, worldbuilding, writing scenes, and so on.

I also offer three multi-lesson courses for writers who are serious about publishing your work:

- **How to Think Sideways**: Career Survival School for Writers
- **How to Revise Your Novel**: How to Get the Book You WANT from the Wreck you Wrote.
- **How to Write a Series**: Master the Art of Episodic Fiction

Not all courses may be available at all times. You can always find what I'm currently offering here:

http://howtothinksideways.com/writing-courses

My Novels, Short Stories, and More

I've written a lot of books in a number of genres: science fiction, fantasy, young adult, suspense, and "defies classification."

I've reissued a number of my books that were out of print for years, and am writing and publishing new work currently.

To find my currently available works, go here:

http://hollylisle.com/new-works-and-reprints

And to get news on when I have a new novel or collection coming out, sign up here:

http://hollylisle.com/the-fun-with-teeth-sign-up-page

Made in the USA
San Bernardino, CA
01 July 2013